REVISE M2

for MEI Structured Mathematics

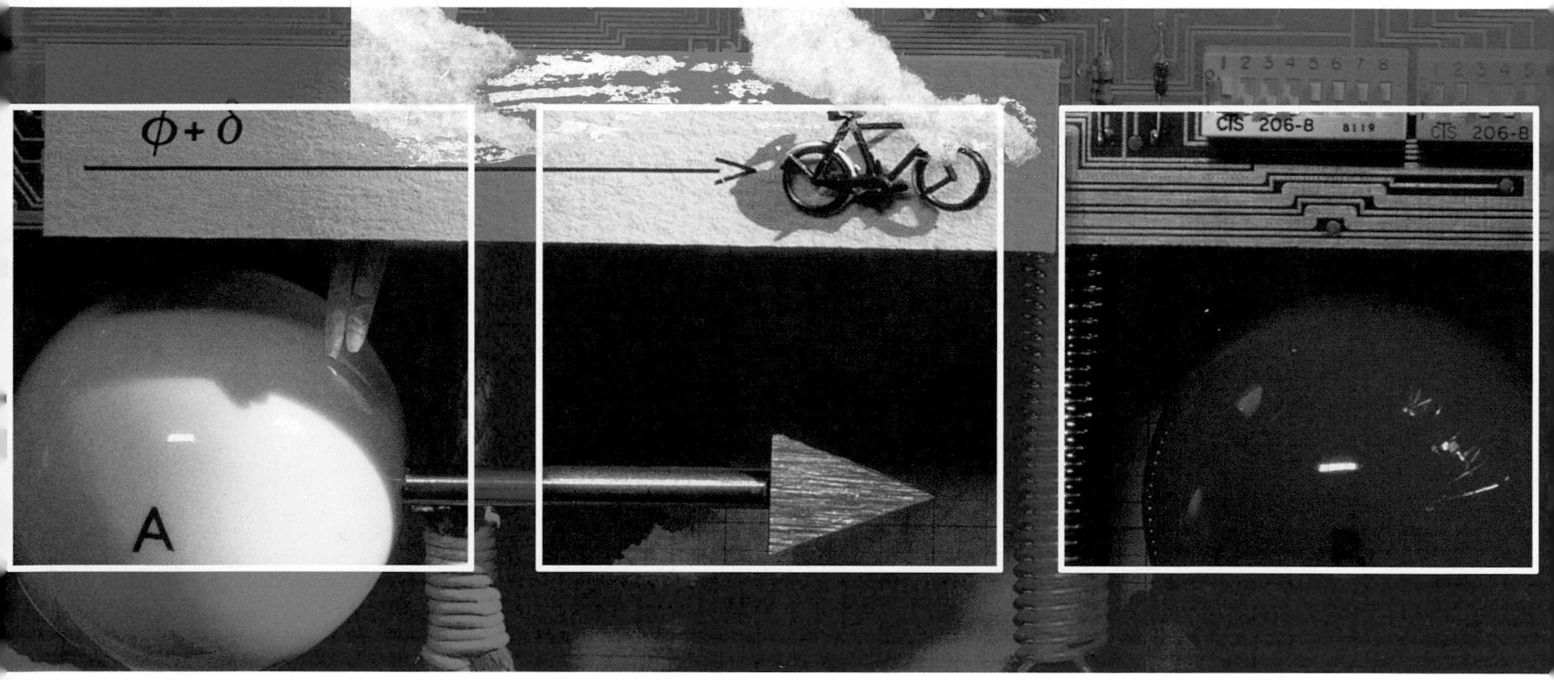

Series Editor
Roger Porkess

Authors
Catherine Berry, John Berry, Sophie Goldie, Stephen Lee, Maureen Sheehan, David Smart and Charlie Stripp

HODDER EDUCATION
AN HACHETTE UK COMPANY

Orders: please contact Bookpoint Ltd, 130 Milton Park, Abingdon, Oxon OX14 4SB.
Telephone: (44) 01235 827720. Fax: (44) 01235 400454. Lines are open 9.00 – 5.00, Monday to Saturday, with a 24-hour message answering service.
Visit our website at www.hoddereducation.co.uk

First published in 2011 by
Hodder Education,
An Hachette UK Company
338 Euston Road
London NW1 3BH

Impression number 5 4 3 2 1
Year 2014 2013 2012 2011

Dynamic Learning Student Online website © Catherine Berry, Sophie Goldie, Richard Lissaman, Charlie Stripp, 2011; with contributions from Tom Carter; developed by MMT Limited; cast: Tom Frankland; recorded at Alchemy Soho.

Typeset in 11/12 Helvetica by Tech-Set Ltd., Gateshead, Tyne & Wear
Printed in Spain

A catalogue record for this title is available from the British Library

ISBN: 978 0 340 957417

Contents

Introduction

Welcome to this Revision Guide for the MEI Mechanics 2 unit!

The book is organised into 14 sections covering the various topics in the syllabus. A typical section is five pages long; the first four pages contain essential information and key worked examples covering the topic. At the start of each chapter, there are page references to where the section topics are covered in the textbook.

The last page in each section has questions for you to answer so that you can be sure that you have really understood the topic. There is a multiple-choice exercise and an exam-style question. If you are to gain the greatest possible benefit from the book, and so do your best in the M2 exam, you should work through these for yourself and then refer to the accompanying website to check your answers.

The multiple-choice questions cover the basic ideas and techniques. It is really important that you work through them carefully; guessing will do you no good at all. When you have decided on the answer you think is right, enter it on the website. If you are right, it tells you so and gives the full solution; check that your answer wasn't just a fluke. If your choice is not right, the website gives you advice about your mistake; the possible wrong answers have all been designed to pick out particular common misunderstandings. The explanations on the website are based on the most likely mistakes; even if you make a different mistake, you will usually find enough help to set you on the right path so that you can try again.

When you come onto the exam-style question, write out your best possible answer. Then go to the website. You will find the solution displayed step-by-step, together with someone talking you through it and giving you helpful advice.

So the book contains the essential information to revise for the exam and, critically, also enables you to check that you have understood it properly. That is a recipe for success.

Finally, a word of warning. This book is designed to be used together with the textbook and not as a replacement for it. This Revision Guide will help you to prepare for the exam but to do really well you also need the deep understanding that comes from the detailed explanations you will find in the textbook.

Good learning and good luck!

Catherine Berry, John Berry, Sophie Goldie, Stephen Lee, Maureen Sheehan, David Smart, Charlie Stripp

Where you see the following icon DL, please refer to the Dynamic Learning Student Online website. Information on how to access this website is printed on the inside front cover of the book.

Accompanying books

MEI Structured Mathematics M2
ISBN 978 0 340 88852 0

Companion to Advanced Mathematics and Statistics
ISBN 978 0 340 95923 7

A model for friction

1

Friction

▶▶ 4

A ABOUT THIS TOPIC

In your work on equilibrium and motion of particles in Mechanics 1, you either used the modelling assumption that surfaces are smooth, so that there is no frictional force, or you were told the frictional force. In this section, you will use a model to work out the frictional force.

R REMEMBER

- Forces and resolution of forces from M1.
- Conditions for equilibrium under a set of concurrent forces from M1.
- Newton's laws of motion from M1.

K KEY FACTS

- The coefficient of friction between two surfaces is a measure of the roughness of the contact between the surfaces, and is usually denoted by μ. If $\mu = 0$, the contact is perfectly smooth and there is no frictional force.
- The frictional force, F, between two surfaces is given by $F \leqslant \mu R$, where R is the normal reaction force between the surfaces.
- When $F = \mu R$, friction is limiting, and the object is either sliding or is on the point of sliding.

Frictional force

When an object is at rest on a rough surface, the frictional force F is given by $F \leqslant \mu R$, where R is the normal reaction of the surface on the object.

If the object has no tendency to move, for example if it is resting on a horizontal surface with no external forces acting on it, the frictional force is zero.

If the object is at rest but has a tendency to move, for example if it lies on a slope, the frictional force opposes the potential motion and its magnitude is just sufficient to prevent the object from moving.

However, the frictional force has a maximum possible value of μR, and the object will move if this maximum value is not sufficient to prevent the movement. In cases where $F = \mu R$, the object is on the point of moving. The friction is described as *limiting*.

EXAMPLE 1

A box of mass 10 kg is pulled along a floor by a horizontal force of 100 N. The coefficient of friction between the box and the floor is 0.8. Find the acceleration of the box.

SOLUTION

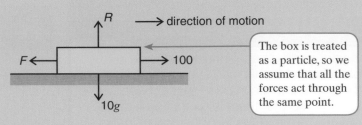

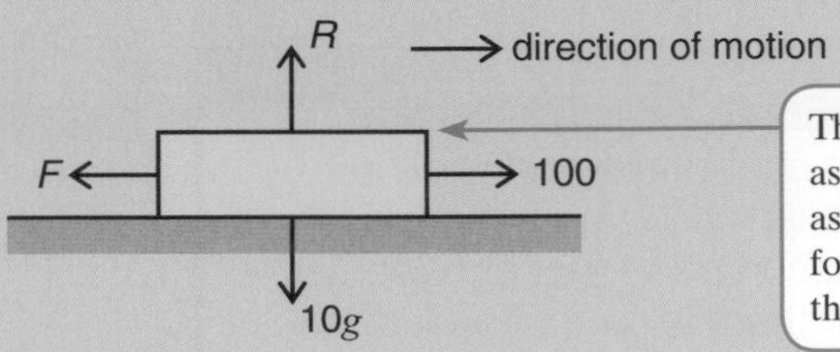

The box is treated as a particle, so we assume that all the forces act through the same point.

Vertically: $R - 10g = 0$

$R = 10g = 98$

Since the block is moving, friction is limiting: $F = \mu R$

$= 0.8 \times 98$

$= 78.4$

Horizontally: $100 - F = 10a$

$100 - 78.4 = 10a$

$21.6 = 10a$

$a = 2.16$

The acceleration of the block is $2.16\,\text{m s}^{-2}$.

The direction of the frictional force

The frictional force always opposes any tendency to motion. This is illustrated in Example 2 below. In part **i)**, the block is tending to slip down the plane, and so the frictional force acts up the plane. In part **ii)**, the block is moving up the plane, so the frictional force opposes this motion and acts down the plane.

EXAMPLE 2

A block of mass 2 kg rests on a plane which is inclined at 20° to the horizontal. The coefficient of friction between the plane and the block is 0.2. The block is held in place by a string parallel to the plane.

i) What is the minimum tension in the string needed to hold the block in place?

ii) What is the tension in the string if the block is on the point of moving up the plane?

SOLUTION

Let the tension in the string be T N.

i) When the minimum tension is applied, the block is about to slide down the plane, so friction is limiting and acts up the plane.

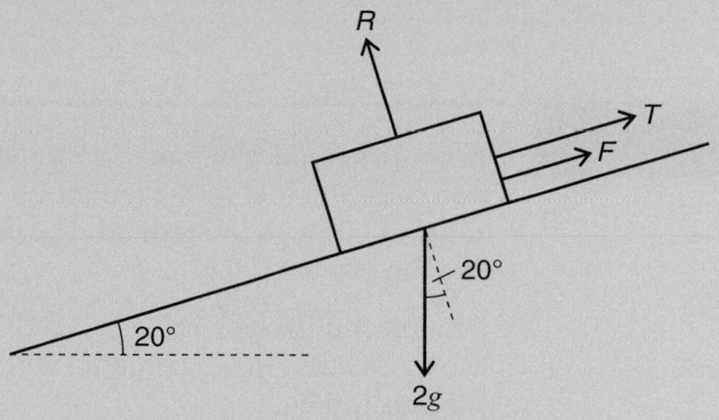

Perpendicular to plane: $R - 2g\cos 20° = 0$

$R = 19.6\cos 20°$

Friction is limiting: $F = \mu R$

$= 0.2 \times 19.6\cos 20°$

$= 3.92\cos 20°$

Parallel to plane: $T + \mathrm{F} - 2g\sin 20° = 0$

$T = 19.6\sin 20° - 3.92\cos 20°$

$T = 3.02$

The minimum tension required is 3.02 N (3 s.f.).

ii) When the block is about to slide up the plane, friction is limiting and acts down the plane.

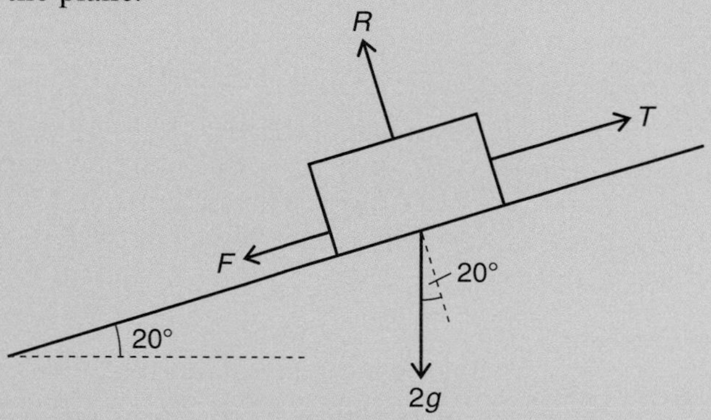

There is no change in the forces perpendicular to the plane, so the magnitude of the frictional force is the same as in part **i)**.

Parallel to plane: $T - F - 2g\sin 20° = 0$

$T = 19.6\sin 20° + 3.92\cos 20°$

$T = 10.4$

The tension is 10.4 N (3 s.f.).

A model for friction

Some examination questions about friction involve the equilibrium of a rigid body, rather than a body which can be treated as a particle. Remember that for a rigid body to be in equilibrium, the total moment of the forces acting on the body must be zero, and the total resultant force must also be zero.

EXAMPLE 3

A uniform ladder of mass 20 kg and length 3 m is placed against a smooth wall, with the foot of the ladder on rough ground. The ladder makes an angle of 60° with the ground. The coefficient of friction between the ladder and the ground is 0.4.

An object of weight W N is placed on a step 50 cm from the top of the ladder. What is the maximum value that the weight can take without the ladder slipping?

SOLUTION

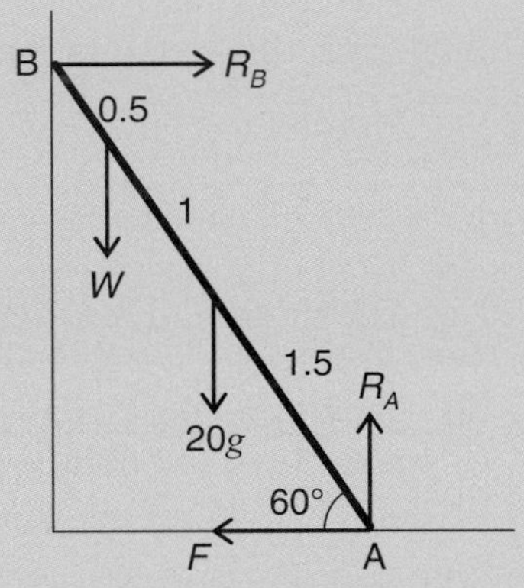

Resolving vertically: $R_A - W - 20g = 0$

$$R_A = W + 196$$

Friction is limiting: $F = \mu R_A$

$$= 0.4(W + 196)$$

$$= 0.4W + 78.4$$

Taking moments about B (↶ +ve):

$$W \cos 60° \times 0.5 + 20g \cos 60° \times 1.5 + F \sin 60° \times 3 - R_A \cos 60° \times 3 = 0$$

$$0.25W + 147 + 3 \sin 60° \,(0.4W + 78.4) - 1.5(W + 196) = 0$$

$$0.25W - 1.5W + 1.2W \sin 60° = 294 - 147 - 235.2 \sin 60°$$

$$W = \frac{147 - 235.2 \sin 60°}{1.2 \sin 60° - 1.25}$$

$$W = 269$$

The maximum value that the weight can take is 269 N (3 s.f.).

LINKS

Friction	Chapter 3 of this unit, when considering equilibrium problems involving rigid bodies such as ladders.
Frictional force	Chapter 5 of this unit.

Test Yourself

1 A block of mass 5 kg is to be pulled along a rough horizontal floor by a rope inclined at 40° to the horizontal. The coefficient of friction between the block and the floor is 0.6. What is the tension in the rope when the block is on the point of moving?

A 25.5 N **B** 32.4 N **C** 38.4 N **D** 2.6 N

2 A particle is placed on a rough plane inclined at 50° to the horizontal. The coefficient of friction between the particle and the plane is 0.4. The particle is pulled up the slope with acceleration $2\,\text{m}\,\text{s}^{-2}$ by a constant force P N which acts parallel to the plane. What is the value of P?

A 14.0 **B** 20.1 **C** 24.1 **D** 22.6

3 A uniform beam AB of length 5 m and weight 50 N is placed with end A resting against a smooth vertical wall and end B resting on rough horizontal ground. The minimum value of the angle that the beam can make with the horizontal without slipping is 40°. What is the value of the coefficient of friction between the beam and the ground?

A 0.420 **B** 1.26 **C** 1.19 **D** 0.596

Exam-Style Question

A uniform beam AB of weight 40 N and length 2 m is placed with end A resting on a smooth horizontal surface, supported by a fixed peg at point P, where BP = 0.6 m. The beam is at an angle of 30° to the horizontal and is on the point of sliding.

i) Draw a diagram showing all the forces acting on the beam.

ii) Explain why the peg at P cannot be smooth.

iii) Find the normal reaction of the peg on the beam at P.

iv) Find in exact form the coefficient of friction between the peg and the beam.

3 Moments of forces

26
27
40, 54

Moments of perpendicular force

A ABOUT THIS TOPIC

In Mechanics 1 the mechanics you learnt was restricted to particles; you treated every object as if it was a point. In this section you take the step of developing the techniques of moments so that you can allow for the shapes that objects actually have.

R REMEMBER

- Forces from M1.
- Equilibrium from M1.

K KEY FACTS

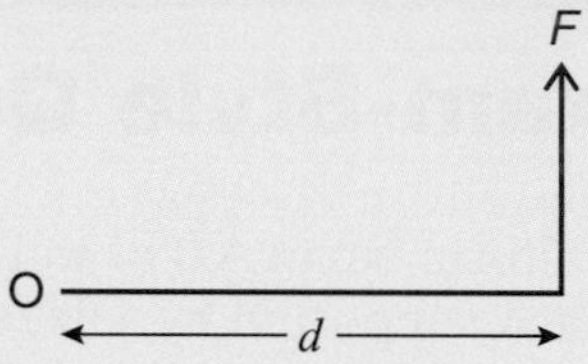

- The moment of a force F about a point O is given by the product Fd where d is the perpendicular distance from O to the line of action of the force.
- The S.I. unit for the moment of a force is the newton metre (Nm).
- A rigid body is only in equilibrium if
  - there is no resultant force acting on it
  - there is no resultant moment about any point.
- When solving a problem you can take moments about any point, but try to find the point that gives you the simplest calculations.

The particle model and the rigid body model

In the particle model, an object is represented by a single particle. You are not concerned with turning forces because the object has no dimensions.

In the rigid body model, an object is represented as a shape, with dimension(s). You need to consider the turning forces on the object.

Forces on a rigid body

Suppose that you push a book that is lying on a smooth desk equally hard in the same direction with one finger of each hand, as shown in this next figure.

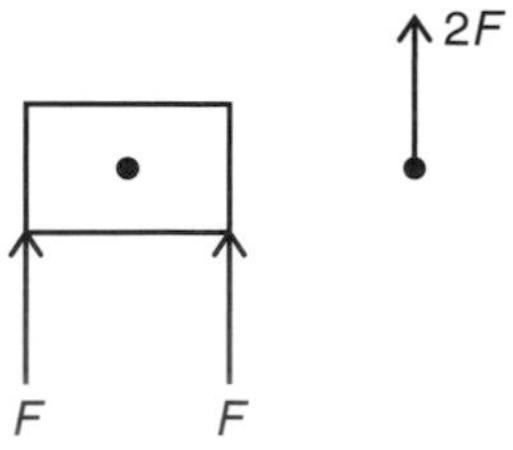

Perhaps you'd like to try this using your M2 Revision Guide?

You would find that the book travels in a straight line in the direction of the applied force.

Now consider a different situation, as shown in this next figure. The book now will not travel in a straight line.

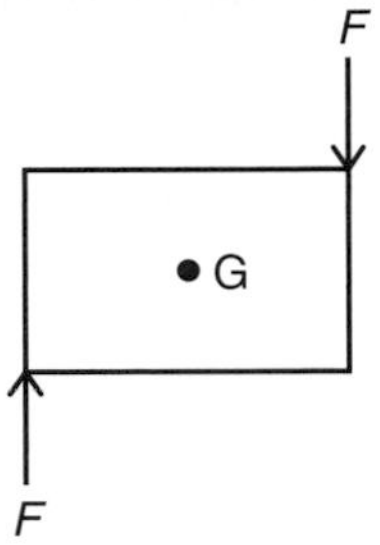

The resultant force on the book is now zero, as the two forces are equal in magnitude but in opposite directions. However, you know from experience that if you actually did this then the book would rotate.

This is an example of a turning effect on an object and is one reason why you need to understand and use moments.

The situation in this figure describes a *couple*. This is where a set of forces, like those above, have a zero resultant but a non-zero total moment. The effect is to cause a rotation of the rigid body.

EXAMPLE 1

In the diagram the point G is 15 cm from AB and 15 cm from CD.

Forces of 4 N act along AB and CD.
Find the total moment about G.

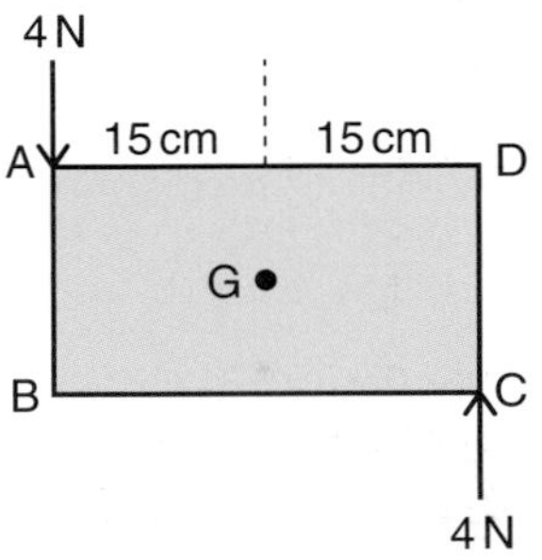

SOLUTION

Anticlockwise (↺ +ve):

Moment of force along AB about G = 4×0.15 Nm anticlockwise

Moment of force along CD about G = 4×0.15 Nm anticlockwise

Total moment about G = $4 \times 0.15 + 4 \times 0.15$
$= 1.2$

So total moment about G is 1.2 Nm anticlockwise.

15 cm = 0.15 m

Notice that the S.I. unit for moment is the newton metre.

Remember that the moment is Fd, where d is the distance; here $d = 0.15$ m.

Moments are always taken about a point and so you must always specify what that point is.

In two dimensions, the sense of a moment is described as either positive (anticlockwise) or negative (clockwise), so in Example 1 the 1.2 Nm moment has a positive sense.

EXAMPLE 2

The situation below shows several forces acting on an object. Find the total moment about the point O and state whether it acts in a clockwise or anticlockwise sense.

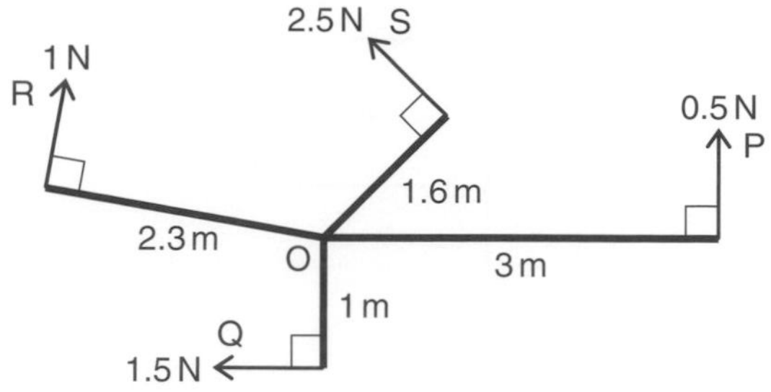

SOLUTION

Anticlockwise (↺ +ve):

Moment of P about O $= 0.5 \times 3$ Nm anticlockwise
Moment of Q about O $= 1.5 \times 1$ Nm clockwise
Moment of R about O $= 1 \times 2.3$ Nm clockwise
Moment of S about O $= 2.5 \times 1.6$ Nm anticlockwise

Total moment about O $= 0.5 \times 3 - 1.5 \times 1 - 1 \times 2.3 + 2.5 \times 1.6$
$= 1.7$

So total moment about O is 1.7 Nm.
The 1.7 Nm acts in the anticlockwise sense.

Remember to include all forces in the calculation. Here there are four forces.

By convention anticlockwise moments are often described as positive.

Equilibrium (for a rigid body model)

In the particle model, which you met in Mechanics 1, an object is in equilibrium if the resultant force on it is zero. In the rigid body model this may not be true, as the forces may not all act through a point.

R RULE

If a rigid body is in equilibrium two conditions apply. There is
- no resultant force and
- no resultant moment about any point.

EXAMPLE 3

A uniform horizontal wooden board of weight 125 N has length 3 m and rests in equilibrium on two vertical supports 10 cm and 260 cm from the left-hand end. What is the magnitude of the reaction force at each of the supports?

SOLUTION

Draw a suitable diagram, showing the forces acting on the wooden board.

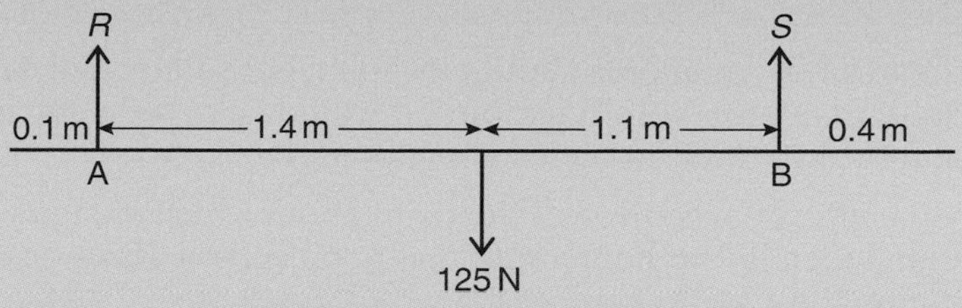

Taking moments about the point A (⟲ +ve):

$$(1.4 + 1.1) \times S - 1.4 \times 125 = 0$$

$$S = \frac{1.4 \times 125}{1.4 + 1.1} = 70$$

Resolving vertically (↑ +ve): $R + S - 125 = 0$

Substituting $S = 70$

$$\Rightarrow \quad R = 125 - 70 = 55$$

Hence, the reaction forces are 55 N at A and 70 N at B.

In this example you took moments about A. Now try it for yourself taking moments about B and check you get the same answer. What happens if you take moments about the mid-point of the board instead?

EXAMPLE 4

The situation opposite shows five forces acting on an object. The object is in equilibrium. Find the values of X, Y and Z.

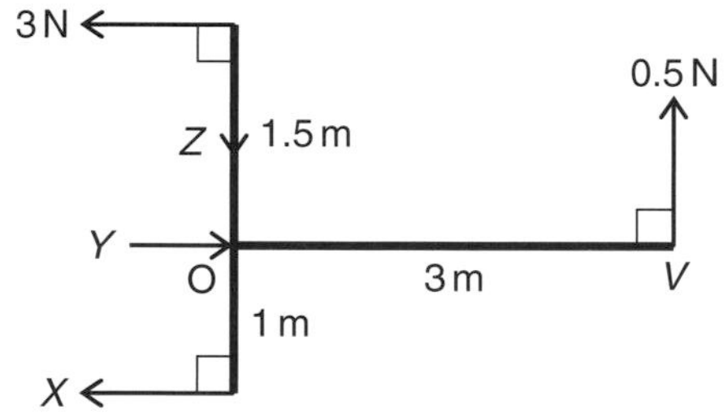

SOLUTION

Anticlockwise (⟲ +ve)

Moment of 0.5 N about O = 0.5 × 3 Nm anticlockwise
Moment of 3 N about O = 3 × 1.5 Nm anticlockwise
Moment of X about O = X × 1 Nm clockwise

As forces Y and Z act through point O, the moment about that point for each of these forces is zero.

Total moment about O $= 0.5 \times 3 + 3 \times 1.5 - X \times 1 = 0$ (as in equilibrium)

$$X = 0.5 \times 3 + 3 \times 1.5$$
$$= 6$$

As a value for X has been found it just remains to resolve horizontally and vertically, to find Y and Z respectively.

Resolving horizontally (→ +ve):

$$Y - X - 3 = 0$$
$$Y = X + 3 = 9$$

Resolving vertically (↑ +ve):

$$0.5 - Z = 0$$
$$Z = 0.5$$

So the force X is 6 N, Y is 9 N and Z is 0.5 N.

A ADVICE

You can take moments about any point, but some points are more useful than others! In Example 3 it would have been equally as useful to consider moments about point B.

When a force acts through the point about which moments are being taken its moment about that point is zero. This was the situation in Example 4.

Be careful with the distances. Always draw a large, clear diagram.

LINKS

Mechanics Centres of Mass (M2, M3), Frameworks (M2), Moments of Inertia (M4).

Test Yourself

1 The diagram opposite shows three forces acting on an object. Which of the following is the total moment about the point A, taking anticlockwise as positive?

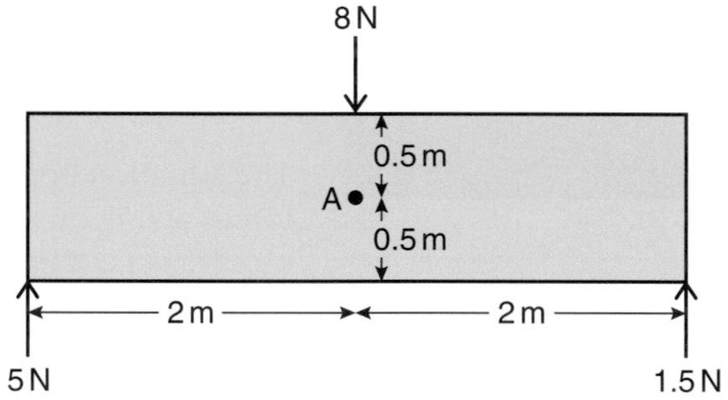

A −7 Nm B −1.5 Nm

C −1.75 Nm D −11 Nm

2 Which of the following is the total moment about the point P, taking anticlockwise as positive?

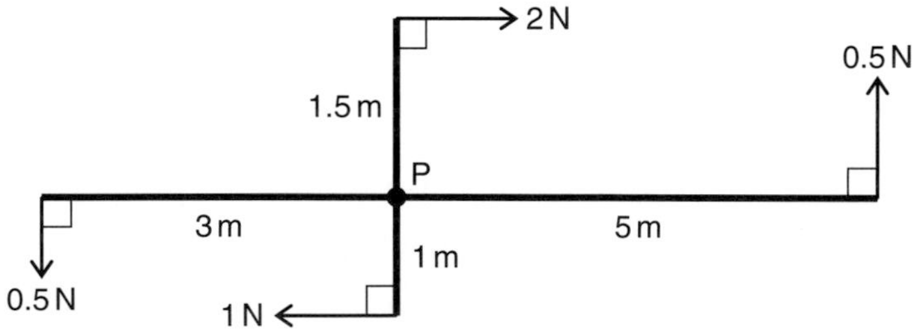

A 8 Nm B 0 Nm C 1 Nm D 4 Nm

3

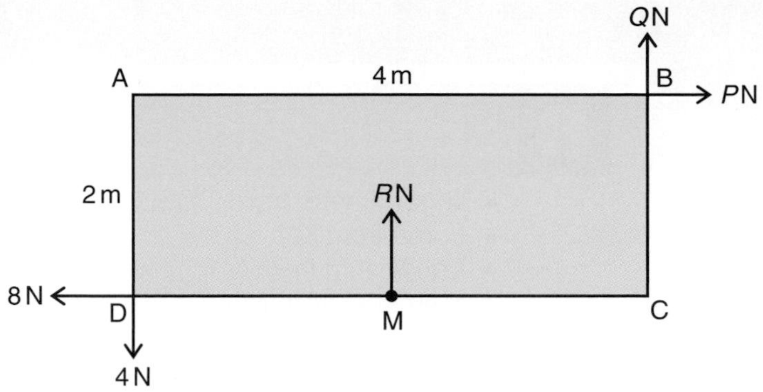

The diagram shows a light, rigid rectangle ABCD. M is the mid-point of DC.
AB = 4 m and AD = 2 m.
Forces 4 N, 8 N, P N, Q N and R N act as shown.
Three of the following statements are false and one is true. Which one is true?

A If $Q = 4$ and $P = 8$, the rectangle is in equilibrium whatever the value of R.

B If $R = 2$, $Q = 2$ and $P = 8$, the rectangle is in equilibrium.

C Given that the rectangle is in equilibrium, the values of P, Q and R depend on what point you take moments about.

D Equilibrium is only possible if $P = 8$, $Q = 4$ and $R = 0$.

Exam-Style Question

A cricket bat from an historic match has length 96 cm and mass 1.4 kg. It is displayed in a museum. It lies horizontally at rest in equilibrium on two vertical supports, which are placed 18 cm and 84 cm from the end of the handle of the bat.

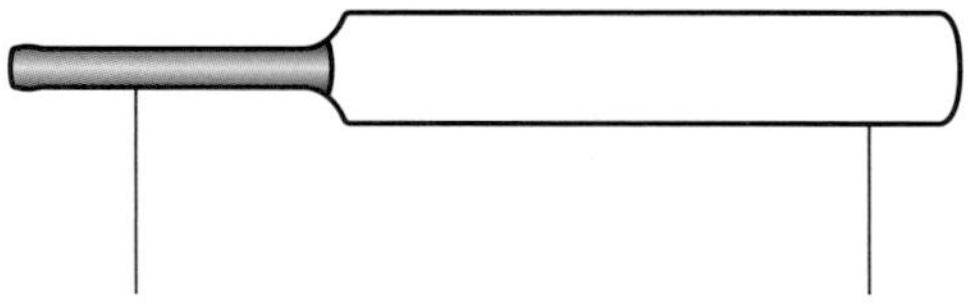

In an initial model, the centre of mass, G, of the bat is taken to be at its middle.

i) Find the magnitude of the reaction force at each of the supports according to this model.

The initial model is not accurate. The supports have been carefully positioned so that the reaction force from each of them is exactly the same.

ii) Find the position of the centre of mass of the bat.

Moments of oblique forces

A ABOUT THIS TOPIC

In the previous section you met the idea of moments, but only for situations involving perpendicular forces. In this section you will develop this idea and consider moments of oblique forces.

R REMEMBER

- Trigonometry from GCSE.
- Force from M1.
- Equilibrium from M1.
- Moments from M2.

K KEY FACTS

- The moment of a force F about a point O is given by the product Fd where d is the perpendicular distance from O to the line of action of the force. So, in the figure on the left, the moment $Fd = Fa \sin \alpha$.

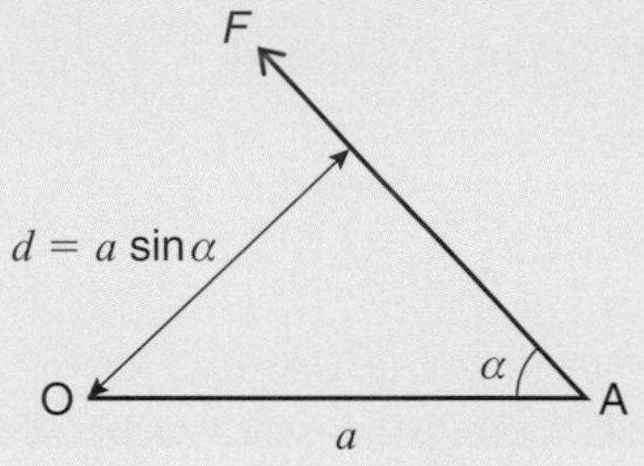

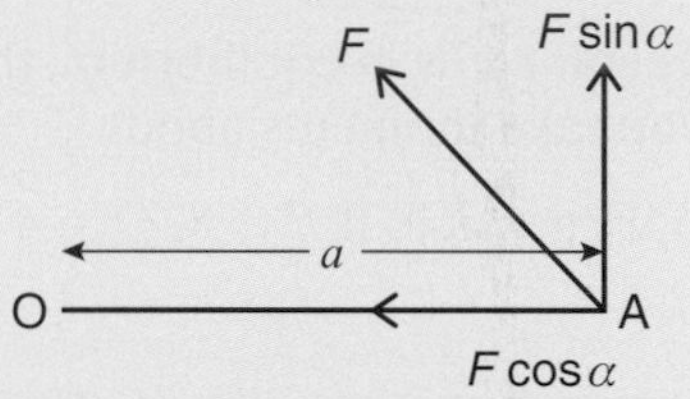

- Another way of looking at the situation is shown in the figure on the right, where F is resolved into components $F \sin \alpha$ perpendicular to OA and $F \cos \alpha$ in the direction AO. The moment about O is $F \sin \alpha \times a + F \cos \alpha \times 0 = Fa \sin \alpha$.
- Sometimes it is easier to use 'Force × perpendicular distance' and other times resolving the force makes your working easier.

EXAMPLE 1

The diagram shows a laptop computer ABCD on display on a horizontal shelf in a shop. AB is 30 cm and AD is 40 cm. Andy is interested in buying the laptop but wants to check what slots there are on the back of the laptop, so he applies the forces of 6 N at D and B at 60° to the computer, as shown in the diagram. What is the total moment about H?

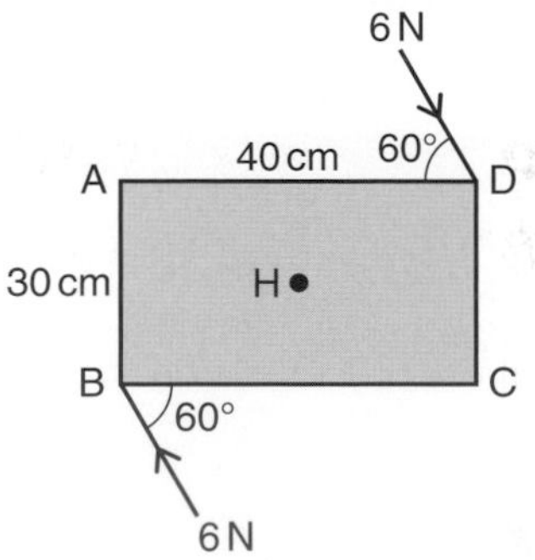

SOLUTION

Start by resolving the 6 N forces in the directions of the edges of the laptop.

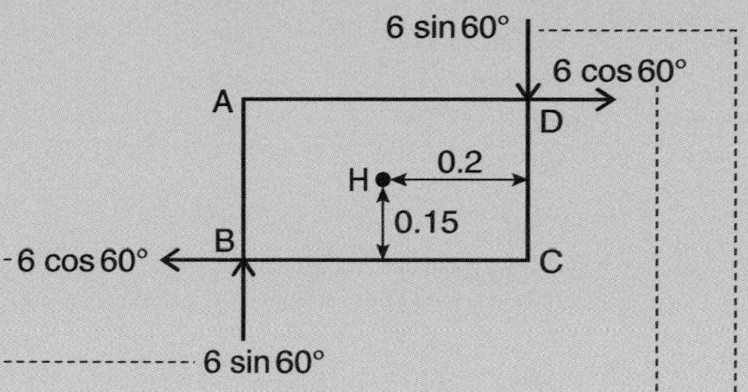

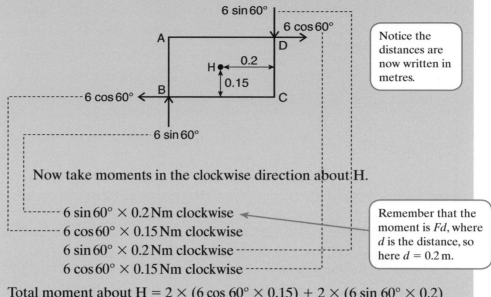

Notice the distances are now written in metres.

Now take moments in the clockwise direction about H.

$6 \sin 60° \times 0.2$ Nm clockwise
$6 \cos 60° \times 0.15$ Nm clockwise
$6 \sin 60° \times 0.2$ Nm clockwise
$6 \cos 60° \times 0.15$ Nm clockwise

Remember that the moment is Fd, where d is the distance, so here $d = 0.2$ m.

Total moment about H $= 2 \times (6 \cos 60° \times 0.15) + 2 \times (6 \sin 60° \times 0.2)$
$= 2.978\ldots$

So total moment about H is 2.98 Nm to 3 s.f.

A ADVICE

In this example, it is a bit messy to calculate the perpendicular distance from H to the lines of action of the forces. By splitting these two forces into components and then taking moments, about point H, for both components of both forces, the overall calculation was simplified.

EXAMPLE 2

Richard is lifting the end P of a uniform heavy plank OP. The other end, O, is on rough ground. The diagram shows the situation when he has just lifted the plank and is holding it stationary whilst he takes a rest to get his breath back. The plank is at an angle of 15° to the horizontal and is on the point of moving.

The mass of the plank is 25 kg and its length is 1.8 m. Richard is exerting a force F N at right angles to the plank. Find F.

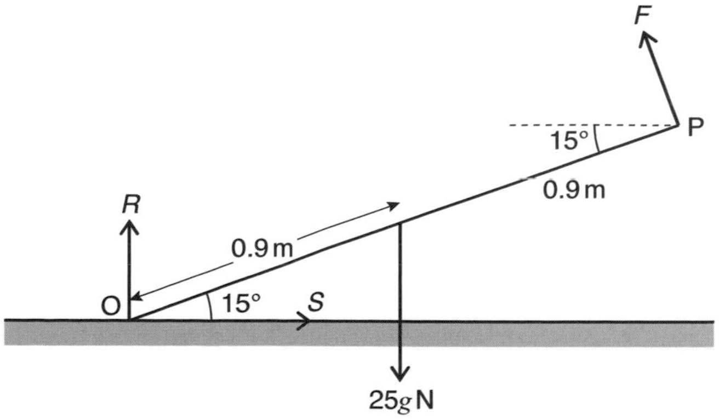

SOLUTION

As you don't know what the reaction is at the ground, take moments about the point of contact, O.

Force F:	$F \times 1.8$	anticlockwise
Weight:	$25g \cos 15° \times 0.9$	clockwise

Since the plank is in equilibrium, the total moment = 0

$F \times 1.8 - 25g \cos 15° \times 0.9 = 0$

$$F = \frac{25g \cos 15° \times 0.9}{1.8} = 118.325\ldots$$

So the force required is 118 N (to 3 s.f.).

A ADVICE

In a situation like this you could have also been asked about the reaction on the ground.

The system is in equilibrium, so you could have found the vertical and horizontal components of the reaction by considering vertical and horizontal equilibrium.

Notice that their resultant, which is the total reaction force, passes through the point where the lines of action of the weight and the lifting force meet, by the triangle of forces rule.

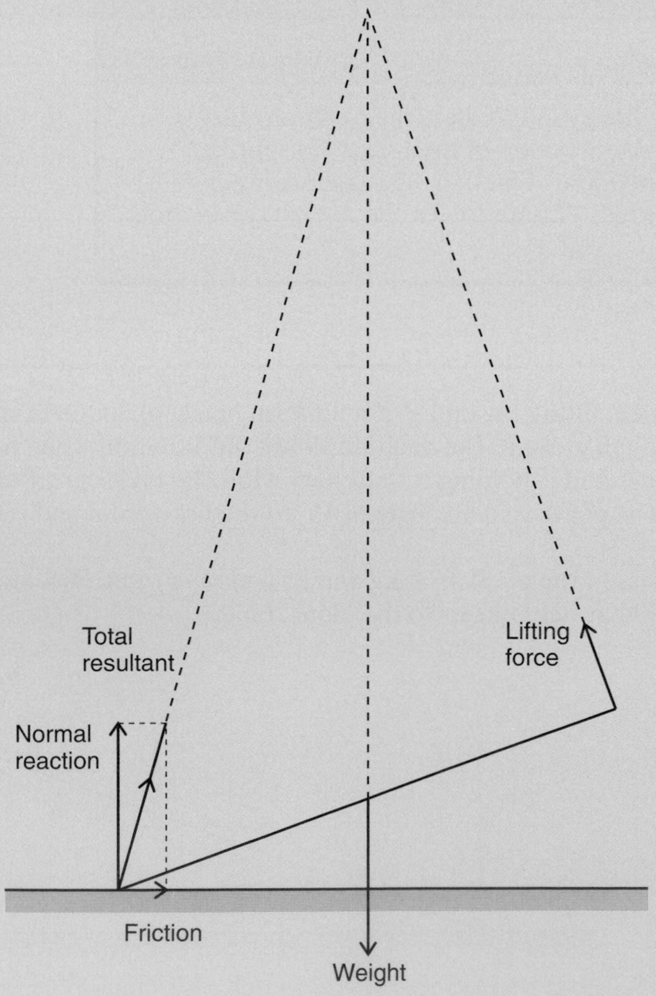

EXAMPLE 3

A uniform ladder of length 2.4 metres, and of mass 24 kg, is placed against the side of a house, so that it makes an angle of 70° with the horizontal. The house is taken to be a smooth surface, but the ground is rough. Find the normal reaction forces at the house and ground and also the frictional force at the ground.

SOLUTION

Start by drawing a diagram. The ladder is AC and B is the bottom of the house. The forces P, Q and R are as shown.

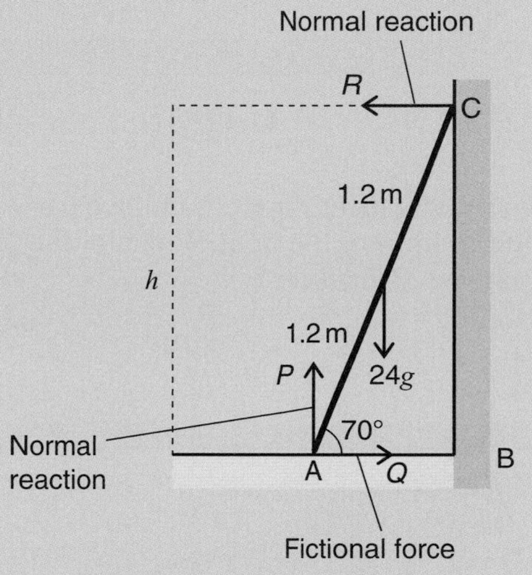

> $h = BC = 2.4 \sin 70°$
> $AB = 2.4 \cos 70°$

As the system is in equilibrium:

Vertical components (↑): $P - 24g = 0$

$$P = 24g = 235.2$$

Horizontal components (→): $Q - R = 0$

$$Q = R \quad ①$$

> This is the distance from A to the line of action of the weight.

Taking moments about the point A (↺ +ve):

$$P \times 0 + Q \times 0 + R \times 2.4 \sin 70° - 24g \times 1.2 \cos 70° = 0$$

$$R = \frac{1.2 \times 24g \cos 70°}{2.4 \sin 70°} = 42.80\ldots$$

> P and Q pass through A so have zero moment about A.

From ① $Q = R = 42.8$ (to 3 s.f.)

The force on the house is 42.8 N, and those on the ground are 42.8 N horizontally and 235.2 N vertically.

LINKS

Mechanics	Centres of Mass (M2, M3), Frameworks (M2), Moments of Inertia (M4).

Test Yourself

1 A uniform plank of length 1.7 metres and of mass 9 kg rests up and over the side of a smooth wall as shown in the diagram below. What is the magnitude of the force P?

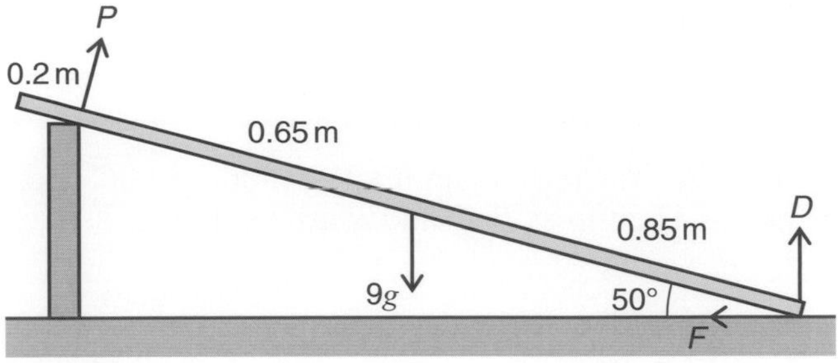

A 32.13 N **B** 137.21 N **C** 49.98 N **D** 38.29 N

2 The diagram shows two people using ropes to pull a narrow boat into the bank of a canal. The point A is a pivot for the motion of the boat. Which of the following is the total moment about the point A, taking anticlockwise as positive?

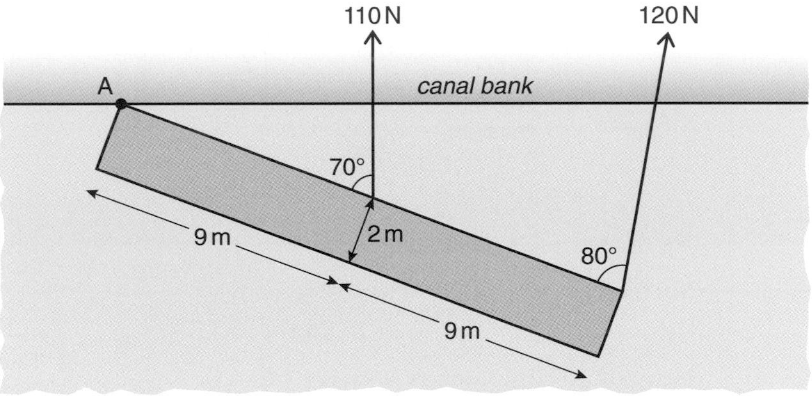

A 222 Nm **B** 714 Nm **C** 3060 Nm **D** 3150 Nm

3 Two children, Ellie and Fatima, are playing and are pushing against a door AB that is hinged at A. The forces they are exerting, and their line of action, are shown on the diagram. The door is being held stationary at an angle of 10° from the closed position, as shown, and is in equilibrium. What is the magnitude of the reaction at the hinge?

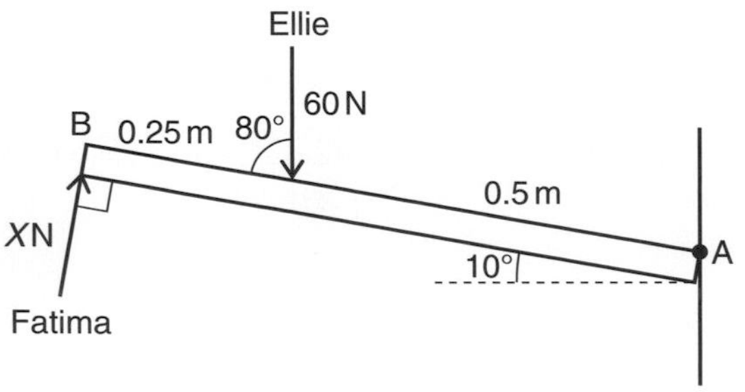

A 6.84 N **B** 22.28 N **C** 65.81 N **D** 20 Nm

Exam-Style Question

Fig. 1 illustrates a model of a girl, Sarah, of mass 57 kg, in position to do a press-up on a horizontal floor.

- Her head is at A, her toes at B, her shoulders at C and her hands at D.
- Her body and legs, AB, and her arms, CD, are straight rigid rods. The centre of mass of AB is at G.
- CD = 52 cm, CB = 140 cm and GB = 95 cm.

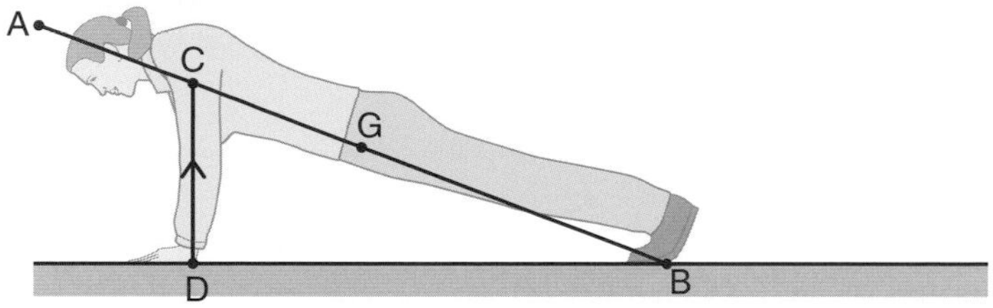

Fig. 1

i) Calculate the force, F N, which Sarah's arms must exert on her body to hold herself in this position.

Sarah now does press-ups on the stairs which are shown in Fig. 2 as a sloping plane at 35° to the horizontal. Her arms are at 90° to the slope. The distances CB and GB are the same as before.

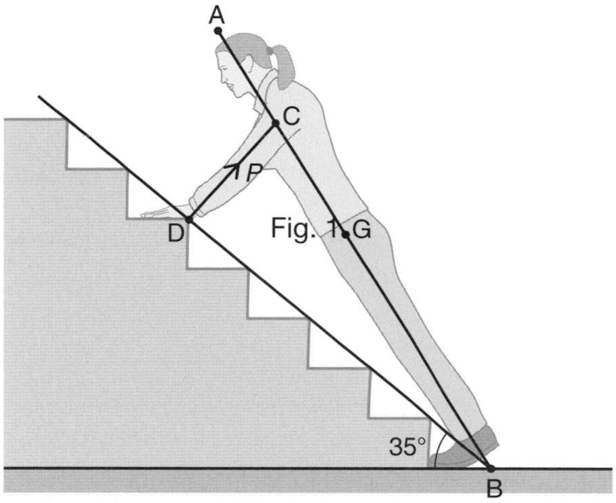

Fig. 2

ii) Calculate the force P N which her arms must exert on her body to hold herself in this position.

Equilibrium, sliding and toppling

A ABOUT THIS TOPIC

When an object is not in equilibrium, a number of things can happen. This section is about two of them, sliding and toppling.

R REMEMBER

- Trigonometry from GCSE.
- Force from M1.
- Equilibrium from M1.
- Moments from M2.

K KEY FACTS

- A body in contact with a plane surface may
  - be in equilibrium and stationary
  - slide
  - topple.
- To solve problems involving sliding and toppling you should resolve forces parallel and perpendicular to the surface.
- The forces may be all or some of
  - the weight
  - the normal reaction
  - the frictional force
  - an applied force.
- When the body is on the point of toppling, the line of action of the normal reaction passes through the pivot point.
- To decide whether a body slides or topples (or neither) work out the conditions, for example, the applied force or the angle of the slope, under which it is
  - on the point of sliding
  - on the point of toppling

  and see which is less severe.

EXAMPLE 1

A uniform cube of mass 6 kg and of length 50 cm is at rest on the floor. A force of K N acts parallel to the floor, along the centre line of the top, as shown in the diagram. The coefficient of friction between the cube and the floor is 0.45. The force is steadily increased. Does the cube slide or topple?

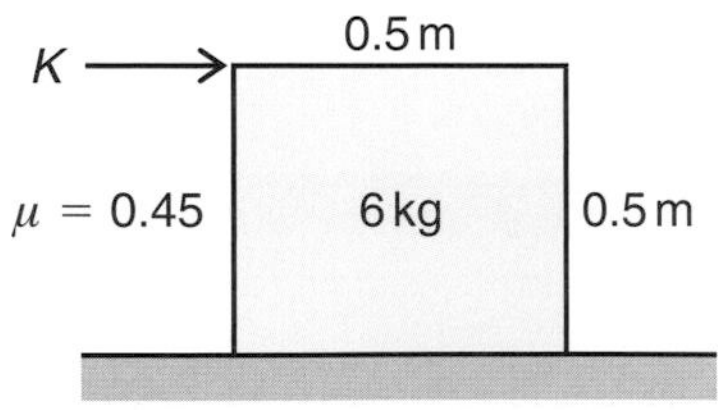

SOLUTION

Find the value of K for which it would just slide and that for which it would just topple.

Sliding:
The cube is in equilibrium until it moves.

Horizontally $K = F$
Vertically $R = 6g$

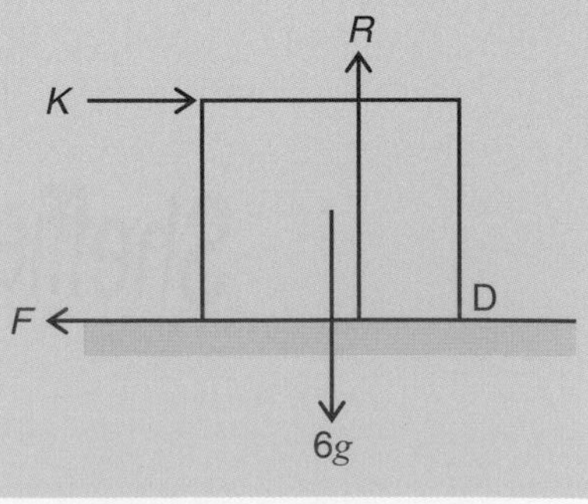

When the cube is on the point of sliding $F = \mu R$

$$= 0.45 \times 6g$$
$$= 26.46$$

So it is on the point of sliding when $K = 26.46$ N.

Toppling:
If the cube is about to topple, then D is the point about which it would pivot. The line of action of R passes through D.

Taking moments about D:

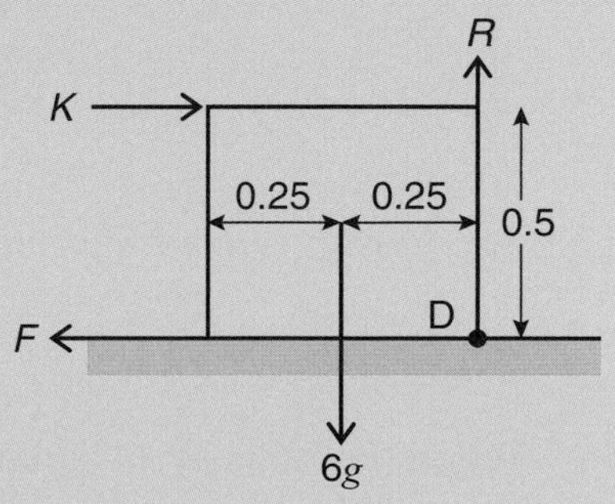

F and R:

The lines of action of F and R both pass though D, so they have zero moment.

K: $K \times 0.5$ clockwise
Weight: $6g \times 0.25$ anticlockwise

Since it is on the point of toppling, the total moment = 0

$$6g \times 0.25 - K \times 0.5 = 0$$
$$K = \frac{6g \times 0.25}{0.5} = 3g$$
$$= 29.4$$

So for the cube to slide, K needs to exceed 26.46 N, but for it to topple K needs to exceed 29.4 N. Therefore the cube slides.

A ADVICE

It is important to understand the two distinctive methods for checking for sliding and toppling. Good clear diagrams are essential.

EXAMPLE 2

A toaster, of mass 2.2 kg lies at rest on a kitchen worktop. The centre of mass of the toaster is in the middle. Prakesh pushes on the toaster with force P N, as shown in the diagram. Will the toaster slide or topple?

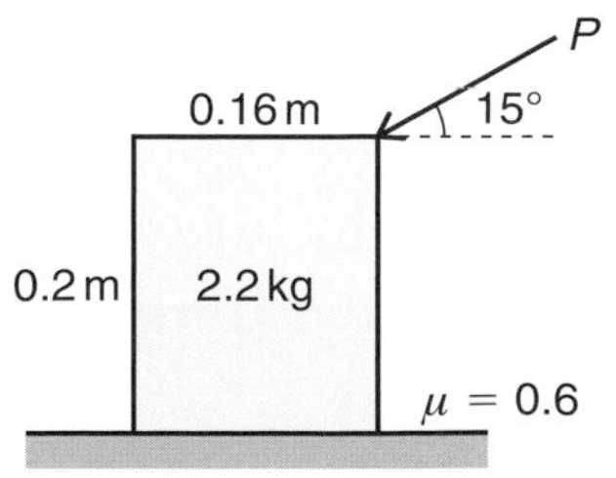

SOLUTION

Find the value of P for which it slides and that for which it just topples.

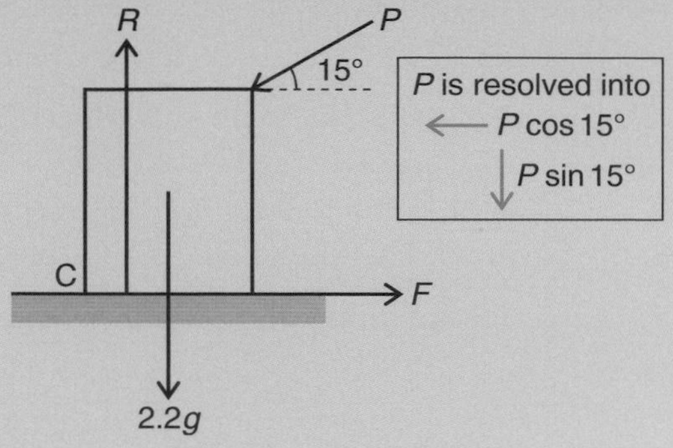

Sliding:

The toaster is in equilibrium until it moves.

Horizontally $P\cos 15° = F$

Vertically $R = 2.2g + P\sin 15°$

When on the point of sliding: $F = \mu R$

$$P\cos 15° = 0.6 \times (2.2g + P\sin 15°)$$

$$P\cos 15° - 0.6 \times P\sin 15° = 0.6 \times 2.2g$$

$$P = \frac{0.6 \times 2.2g}{\cos 15° - 0.6 \times \sin 15°} = 15.957\ldots$$

So it is on the point of sliding when $P = 15.96$ N.

Toppling:

If the toaster is about to topple, then C is the point about which it would pivot. The line of action of R passes through C.

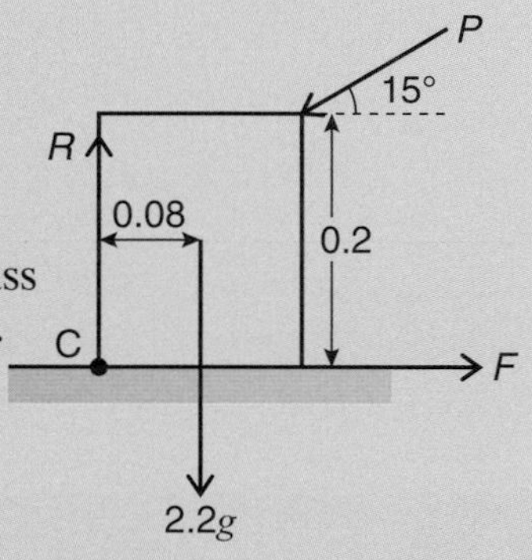

Taking moments about C:

F and R: The lines of action of F and R both pass through C, so they have zero moment.

P: The moments of the resolved component of P are:

$P \times \cos 15° \times 0.2$ anticlockwise

$P \times \sin 15° \times 0.16$ clockwise

Weight: $2.2g \times 0.08$ clockwise

Since it is on the point of toppling, the total moment = 0

$$P \times \cos 15° \times 0.2 - 2.2g \times 0.08 - P \times \sin 15° \times 0.16 = 0$$

$$P \times \cos 15° \times 0.2 - P \times \sin 15° \times 0.16 = 2.2g \times 0.08$$

$$P = \frac{2.2g \times 0.08}{0.2 \times \cos 15° - 0.16 \times \sin 15°} = 11.364\ldots$$

So for the toaster to slide, P needs to exceed 15.96 N, but for it to topple P needs to exceed 11.36 N. Therefore the toaster topples.

EXAMPLE 3

A uniform rectangular object of mass 12 kg is placed on an inclined slope as shown. The coefficient of friction between it and the slope is 0.3. The angle β is gradually increased. When the object is no longer in equilibrium, does it slide or topple?

SOLUTION

Two calculations need to be performed, one to find the angle at which the object would slide and one to find when it would topple.

For both of these, start by resolving the weight into $12g \sin \beta$ parallel to the slope and $12g \cos \beta$ perpendicular to it.

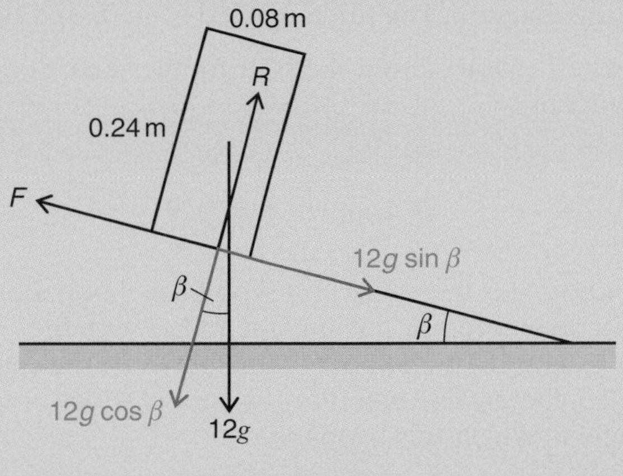

Sliding:
The diagram shows the forces acting when the block is in equilibrium.

Parallel to the slope: $F = 12g \sin \beta$
Perpendicular to slope: $R = 12g \cos \beta$

On the point of sliding $F = \mu R$

$$12g \sin \beta = \mu \times 12g \cos \beta$$
$$\frac{\sin \beta}{\cos \beta} = \frac{\mu \times 12g}{12g}$$
$$\beta = \arctan (0.3) = 16.7°$$

Notice that when it is on the point of toppling, the centre of mass, G, is directly above the pivot point, A.

Toppling:
The diagram on the right shows the forces acting when the block is in equilibrium, but on the point of toppling. Note that all forces, including the weight, act through A, the bottom corner of the object.
The angle β is given by:

$$\tan \beta = \frac{0.08}{0.24}, \beta = 18.4°$$

The angle for toppling (18.4°) is greater than the angle for sliding (16.7°) and so the object slides when $\beta = 16.7°$.

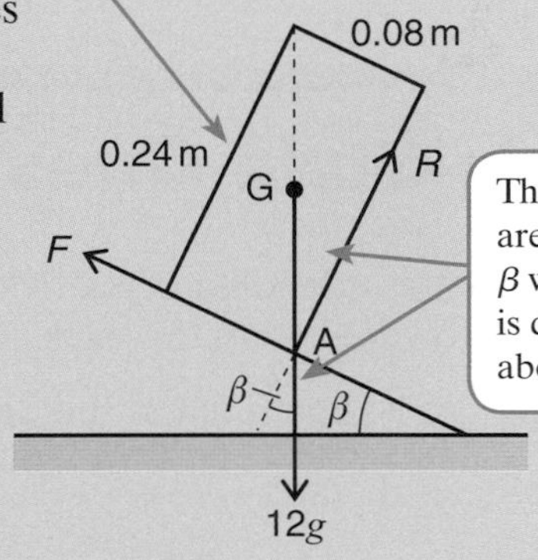

These angles are both β when G is directly above A.

A ADVICE

Notice that although intuitively you may think that a 'tall thin' object would topple before it slides, the coefficient of friction is key to determining whether this is the case. If the coefficient of friction is small enough, it will slide.

LINKS

Mechanics Centres of Mass (M2, M3), Moments of Inertia (M4).

Test Yourself

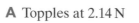

1 A cuboid of mass 800 g is at rest on a rough table. The coefficient of friction is 0.25. Ana pushes the cuboid with her finger. This produces a force of T N which acts parallel to the table and at the top corner, as shown in the diagram. The force applied is increased slowly.

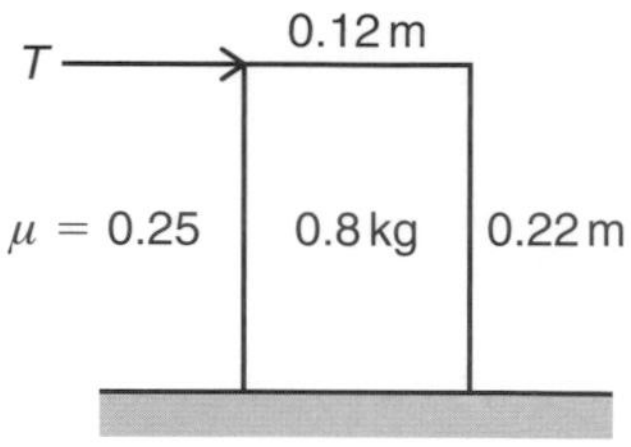

Determine whether the cuboid slides or topples first. State the force when this happens.

A Topples at 2.14 N **B** Slides at 1.96 N

C Slides at 0.2 N **D** Topples at 3.92 N

2 A uniform cuboid has mass 75 g and is on a level horizontal plane. The plane is slowly tilted so the angle it makes with the horizontal is β. The coefficient of friction between the cuboid and the plane is 0.3. Determine whether the cuboid slides or topples. State the angle at which this happens.

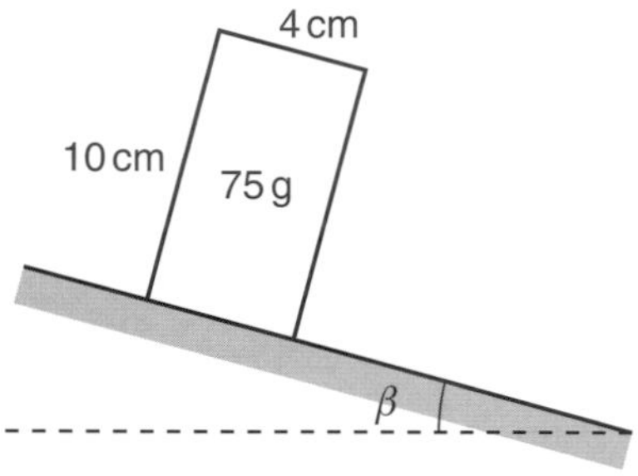

A Slides at 73.3° **B** Topples at 21.8°

C Slides at 16.7° **D** Slides at 17.5°

3 A uniform cuboid, of mass 3 kg, lies at rest on a rough horizontal desk. The coefficient of friction is 0.35. Jamila pushes on it with a force L N, as shown in the diagram. Determine whether the cuboid slides or topples and state the force when this happens.

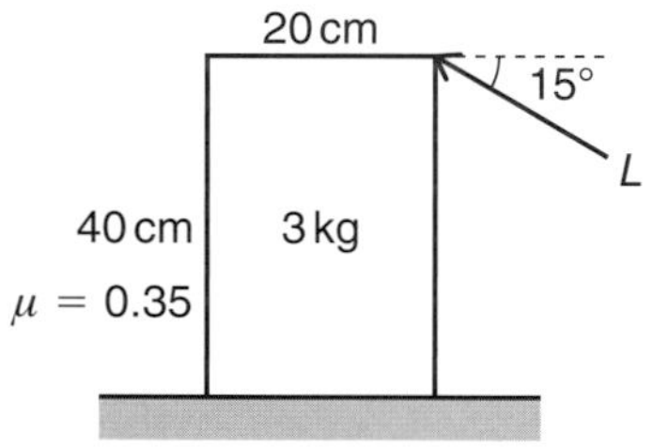

A Slides at 11.76 N **B** Topples at 7.35 N

C Slides at −129.8 N **D** Topples at 8.79 N

Exam-Style Question

Some men are unloading a box from the back of a lorry.
A ramp is lowered from the back of the lorry so the box can slide down it to the ground.

The situation is illustrated in the diagram below.

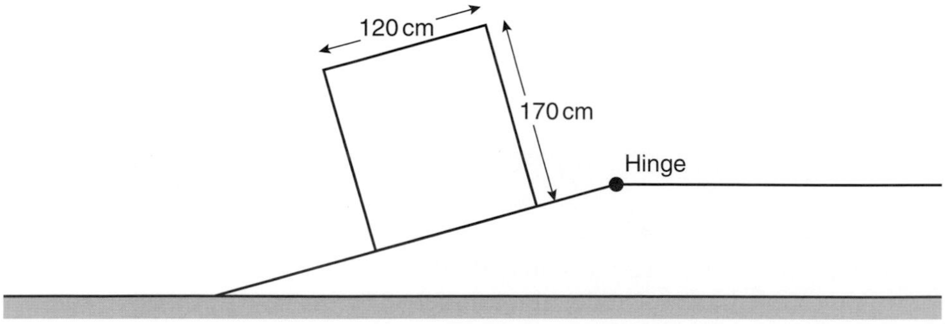

The mass of the box is 150 kg.

The centre of mass of the box is 130 cm above the centre of its base.

The coefficient of friction between the box and the ramp is 0.45.

i) Find the angle at which the box

A) would topple

B) would slide down the ramp.

Which of these happens first?

When the ramp is fully lowered it makes an angle of 25° to the road. The men tie a rope around the middle of the box to prevent it toppling. The rope is parallel to the ramp, as shown in the diagram below.

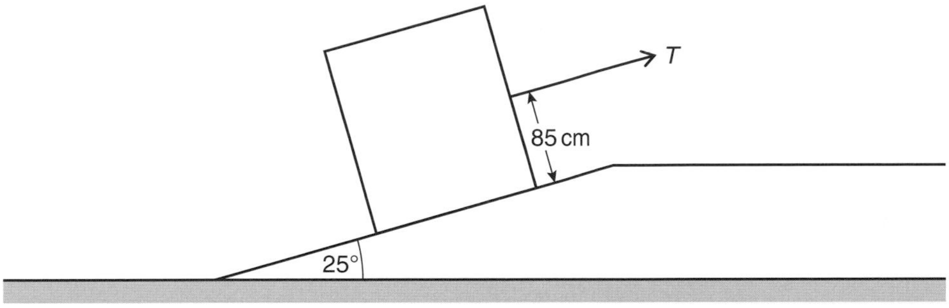

ii) Calculate the minimum tension, T, required in the rope to prevent the box from toppling.

iii) When this minimum tension, T, is applied to the rope, determine whether the box will slide down the ramp.

4 Centre of mass

63
66
70

Centre of mass of uniform and composite bodies

A ABOUT THIS TOPIC

So far you have used the centre of mass as the point in an object through which the line of action of the force of gravity acts. For the particle model, the centre of mass is the single point at which the whole mass of the body may be taken as situated. In the rigid body model, the concept of the centre of mass is the balance point of a body with shape and size.

R REMEMBER

- The definition of moments of forces and the concept of equilibrium from M1.
- The conditions for sliding and toppling from Chapter 3 of M2.

K KEY FACTS

- The centre of mass has the property that the moment, about any point, of the whole mass of the body taken at the centre of mass is equal to the sum of the moments of the various particles comprising the body.
- For a set of n point masses $m_1, m_2, \ldots, m_n$ attached to a rigid light rod at positions $x_1, x_2, \ldots, x_n$ from one end O, the position of the centre of mass relative to O, $\bar{x}$, is given by the equation $M\bar{x} = \sum_{i=1}^{n} m_i x_i$ where M is the total mass.
- For a set of n point masses $m_1, m_2, \ldots, m_n$ distributed in two dimensions located at positions $(x_1, y_1), (x_2, y_2), \ldots (x_n, y_n)$ from an origin O, the position of the centre of mass relative to O, $(\bar{x}, \bar{y})$, is given by the equations

  $M\bar{x} = \sum_1^n m_i x_i$, and $M\bar{y} = \sum_1^n m_i y_i$ where M is the total mass.

  Similarly in three dimensions, $M\bar{z} = \sum_1^n m_i z_i$.
- In 2 and 3 dimensions it is often helpful to use column vectors to set out centre of mass calculations.
- The centre of mass of a composite body is found by modelling it as a system of particles.
- If an object has an axis of symmetry then the centre of mass lies on it.

⚠ It is important to define the position of the origin clearly.

EXAMPLE 1

Four masses are attached to a light rod in the positions shown in the diagram.

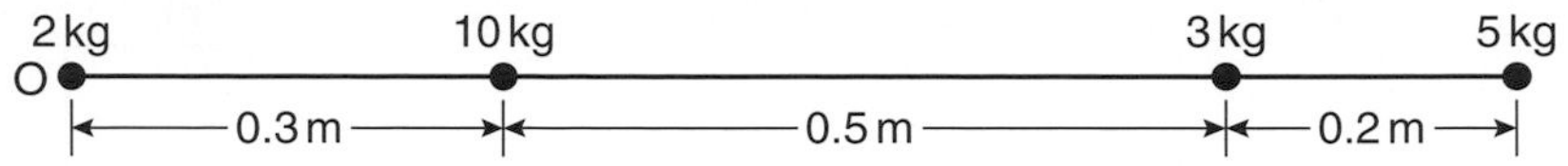

Find the position of the centre of mass of the system from the end O.

SOLUTION

Let the centre of mass be at a distance $\bar{x}$ from O.

R RULE

The moment, about any point, of the whole mass taken to be at the centre of mass equals the sum of the moments of the individual masses about the same point.

This is written as the formula $M\bar{x} = \sum_1^n m_i x_i$.

The whole mass, $M = 2 + 10 + 3 + 5 = 20\,\text{kg}$

Taking moments about O

$20 \times \bar{x} = 2 \times 0 + 10 \times 0.3 + 3 \times 0.8 + 5 \times 1.0$

$20\bar{x} = 10.4$

$\bar{x} = \dfrac{10.4}{20} = 0.52$

So the centre of mass is 0.52 m from the end O.

A ADVICE

In this example, moments were taken about O. You could have taken them about any point. Always try to find the point that will make the work easiest.

The next example reminds you how to model a composite system of objects as a system of particles.

EXAMPLE 2

The diagram gives the dimensions of the design of a uniform metal plate.

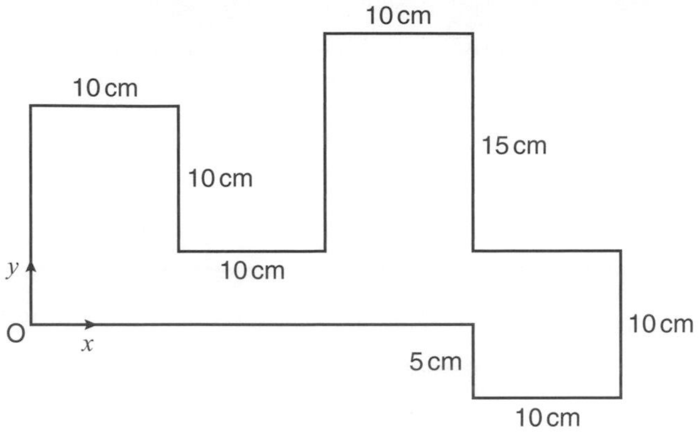

Taking O as the origin and x- and y-axes as shown, find the position of the centre of mass of the plate.

SOLUTION

The first step is to split the plate into four rectangles. The centre of mass of each of these rectangles is at its middle.

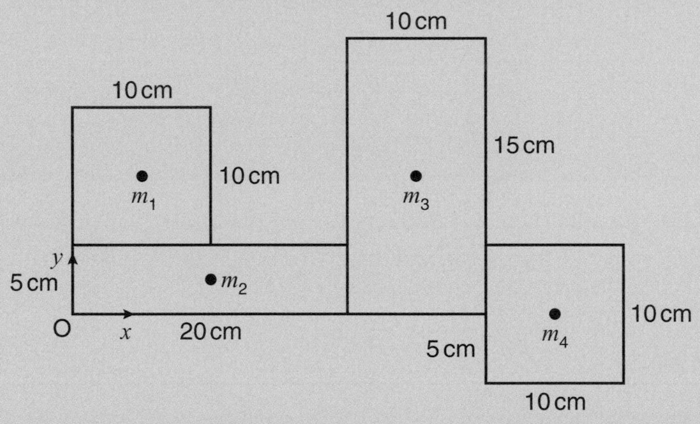

You can model the plate as four point masses m_1, m_2, m_3 and m_4 which are proportional to the areas of the rectangles. Since the areas are 100 cm^2, 100 cm^2, 200 cm^2 and 100 cm^2, the masses in suitable units are 100, 100, 200 and 100, and the total mass is 100 + 100 + 200 + 100 = 500 (mass units). The table below gives the mass and position of m_1, m_2, m_3 and m_4.

Mass	$\boldsymbol{m_1}$	$\boldsymbol{m_2}$	$\boldsymbol{m_3}$	$\boldsymbol{m_4}$	$\boldsymbol{M}$
Mass units	100	100	200	100	500
Position of centre of mass x	5	10	25	35	$\bar{x}$
y	10	2.5	10	0	$\bar{y}$

Take moments about O.
Using column vector notation:

$$500\begin{pmatrix}\bar{x}\\ \bar{y}\end{pmatrix} = 100\begin{pmatrix}5\\ 10\end{pmatrix} + 100\begin{pmatrix}10\\ 2.5\end{pmatrix} + 200\begin{pmatrix}25\\ 10\end{pmatrix} + 100\begin{pmatrix}35\\ 0\end{pmatrix}$$

$$500\begin{pmatrix}\bar{x}\\ \bar{y}\end{pmatrix} = \begin{pmatrix}10\,000\\ 3\,250\end{pmatrix}$$

$$\begin{pmatrix}\bar{x}\\ \bar{y}\end{pmatrix} = \begin{pmatrix}20\\ 6.5\end{pmatrix}$$

The centre of mass is at the point (20, 6.5). Units are cm and the origin is O.

EXAMPLE 3

A child's toy consists of three shapes all cut out of the same uniform lamina as shown in the diagram. The shapes are a circle, a square and an isosceles triangle.

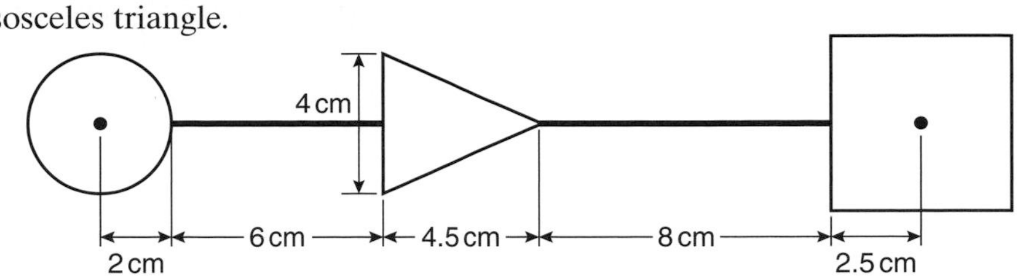

The three shapes are attached to a rigid light rod at the positions shown.

Find the position of the centre of mass.

A child throws the toy across the room. Explain the importance of the centre of mass in describing the motion of the toy.

SOLUTION

The centre of mass lies on the axis of symmetry.
Model the toy as three point masses which are proportional to the areas of the geometrical shapes.
The area of the disc is $\pi \times 2^2 = 4\pi$ mass $= 4\pi$ units
The area of the triangle is $\frac{1}{2} \times 4 \times 4.5 = 9$ mass $= 9$ units
The area of the square is $5^2 = 25$ mass $= 25$ units

The next step is to find the position of the centre of mass of each shape.

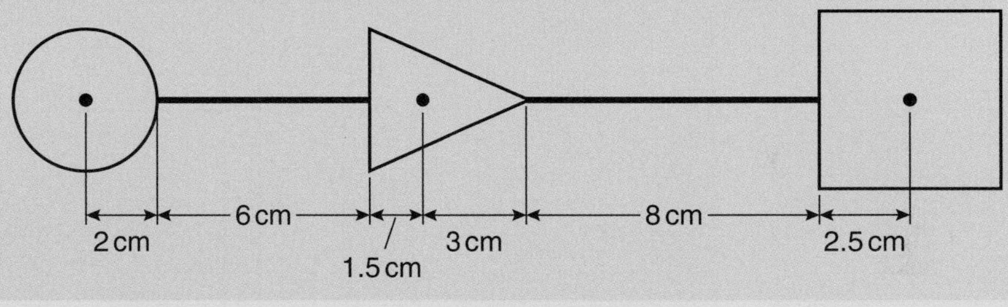

The exam formula booklet tells you that, for a triangular lamina, the centre of mass is $\frac{2}{3}$ of the way along the median from the vertex.

So the position of the centre of mass of the isosceles triangle is $\frac{2}{3} \times 4.5$ cm $= 3$ cm from its vertex.

The position of the centre of mass of each shape is shown in the following diagram.

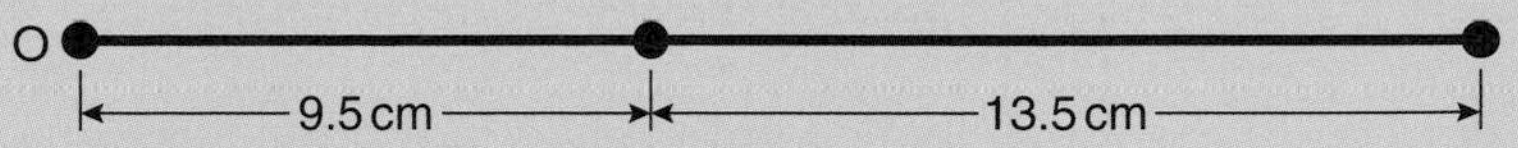

Let the distance of the centre of mass from the centre of the disc O be $\bar{x}$.
Taking moments about O:

$$M\bar{x} = m_1\bar{x}_1 + m_2\bar{x}_2 + m_3\bar{x}_3$$
$$(4\pi + 9 + 25)\bar{x} = (4\pi \times 0) + (9 \times 9.5) + (25 \times 23)$$
$$\bar{x} = 14.18 \text{ to 2 d.p.}$$

The centre of mass is 14.18 cm from O and so 16.18 cm from the end of the toy (i.e. from the edge of the circle).

If the toy is thrown by a child, the centre of mass will move as an ordinary projectile; there will also be spinning motion about the centre of mass.

EXAMPLE 4

Frank is a mathematics teacher who has a large wooden letter F he uses as a paperweight. The letter F is made up of uniform rectangular shapes as shown in the figure. The measurements are in centimetres. The object is 2 cm thick and the density of the wood is $0.8\,\text{g cm}^{-3}$. The letter is mounted on a rectangular stand made from the same material as the letter. The stand is 2 cm thick, 5 cm wide and 15 cm long.

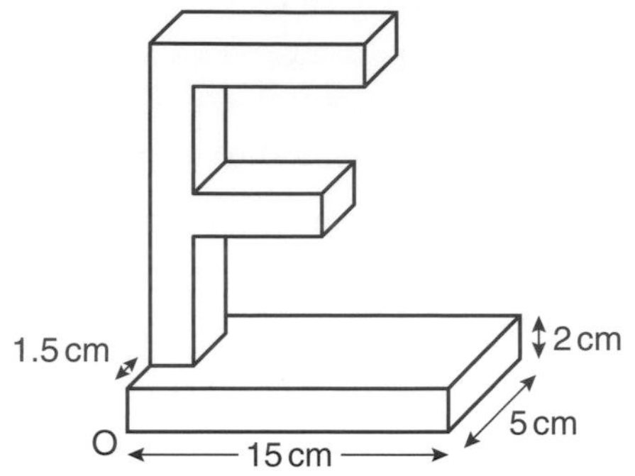

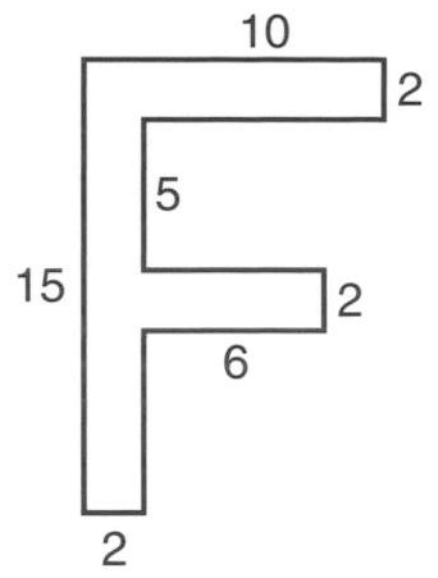

i) Find the mass of the object.

ii) Find the position of the centre of mass from the corner O.

SOLUTION

i) The first step is to split the paperweight into four cuboids A, B, C and the base D. The mass of each cuboid is the product of its volume and density.

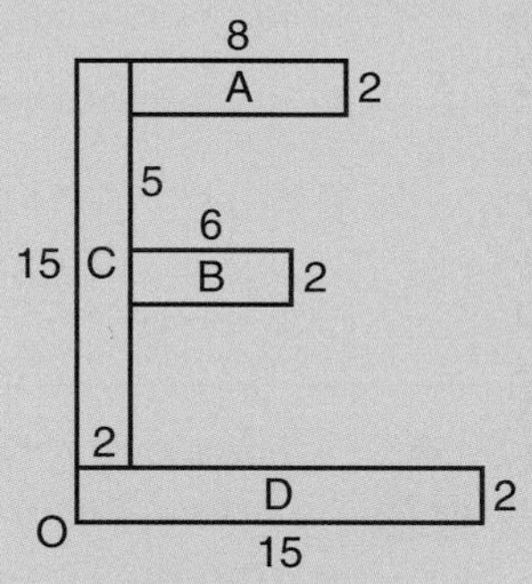

A: The mass is $8 \times 2 \times 2 \times 0.8 = 25.6$ g
B: The mass is $6 \times 2 \times 2 \times 0.8 = 19.2$ g
C: The mass is $2 \times 15 \times 2 \times 0.8 = 48$ g
D: The mass is $15 \times 5 \times 2 \times 0.8 = 120$ g

So the mass of the object is $25.6 + 19.2 + 48 + 120 = 212.8$ g.

ii) Define the x, y and z co-ordinates using corner O as the origin as shown.

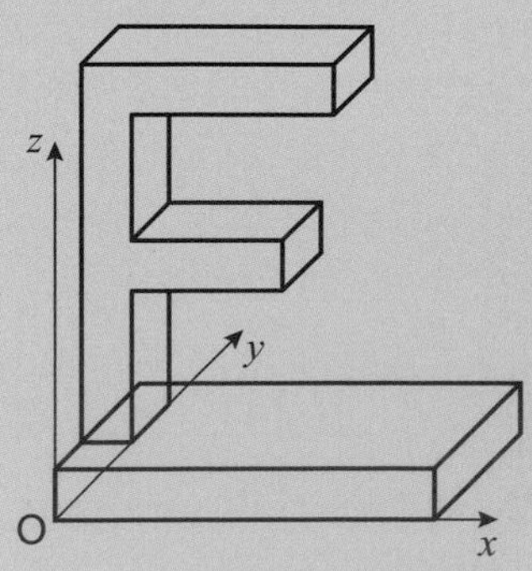

The mass of each cuboid and the centre of mass of each cuboid are shown in the following table:

Cuboid	A	B	C	D	Total mass M
Mass	25.6	19.2	48	120	212.8
Position of the centre of mass $\begin{pmatrix} x \\ y \\ z \end{pmatrix}$	$\begin{pmatrix} 6 \\ 2.5 \\ 16 \end{pmatrix}$	$\begin{pmatrix} 5 \\ 2.5 \\ 9 \end{pmatrix}$	$\begin{pmatrix} 1 \\ 2.5 \\ 9.5 \end{pmatrix}$	$\begin{pmatrix} 7.5 \\ 2.5 \\ 1 \end{pmatrix}$	$\begin{pmatrix} \bar{x} \\ \bar{y} \\ \bar{z} \end{pmatrix}$

Take moments about O to find $\bar{x}, \bar{y}$ and $\bar{z}$

$$212.8 \times \begin{pmatrix} \bar{x} \\ \bar{y} \\ \bar{z} \end{pmatrix} = 25.6 \times \begin{pmatrix} 6 \\ 2.5 \\ 16 \end{pmatrix} + 19.2 \times \begin{pmatrix} 5 \\ 2.5 \\ 9 \end{pmatrix} + 48 \times \begin{pmatrix} 1 \\ 2.5 \\ 9.5 \end{pmatrix} + 120 \begin{pmatrix} 7.5 \\ 2.5 \\ 1 \end{pmatrix}$$

$$212.8 \times \begin{pmatrix} \bar{x} \\ \bar{y} \\ \bar{z} \end{pmatrix} = \begin{pmatrix} 1197.6 \\ 532 \\ 1158.4 \end{pmatrix}$$

$$\begin{pmatrix} \bar{x} \\ \bar{y} \\ \bar{z} \end{pmatrix} = \begin{pmatrix} 5.627\ldots \\ 2.5 \\ 5.443\ldots \end{pmatrix}$$

Is it a surprise that $\bar{y} = 2.5$?

The centre of mass is (5.63, 2.5, 5.44) (to 2 d.p.). Units are cm and the origin is O.

EXAMPLE 5

The diagram shows the design for an earring which consists of a circular disc, centre A and radius 10 mm. A circular hole, centre B and radius 7 mm, is cut from the large circle. The earring is made out of uniform thin material.

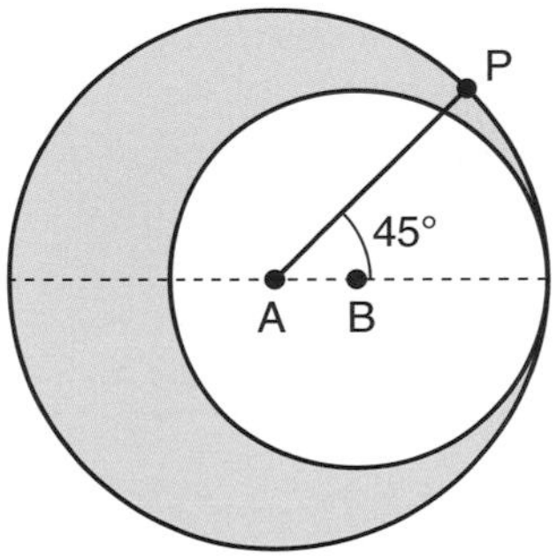

i) Find the position of the centre of mass of the earring.

ii) The earring is hung from an ear by a small light chain attached to the earring at P where angle BAP is 45°. Find the angle that the line AB makes with the vertical.

SOLUTION

i) In a problem like this, think of the original uncut disc as a composite body made up of the earring and a disc which fits into the hole. Since the material is uniform, the mass of each part is proportional to its area. The centre of mass lies on the axis of symmetry AB.

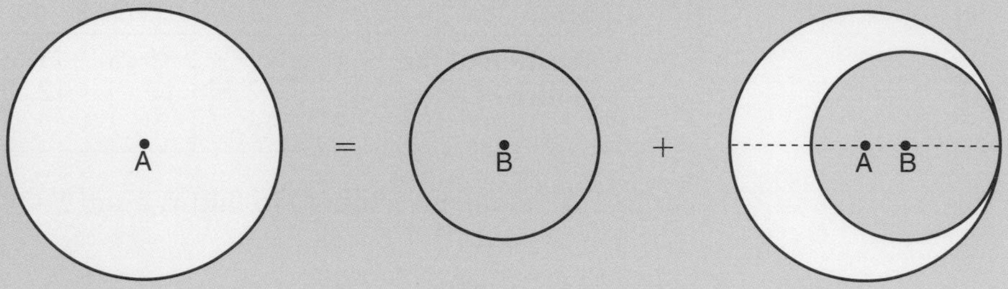

The earring is made out of uniform material so call the density of the material ρ g mm^{-2}.

Shape	**Uncut disc**	**Disc that fits hole**	**Earring**
Area	$\pi \times 10^2 = 100\pi$	$\pi \times 7^2 = 49\pi$	$100\pi - 49\pi = 51\pi$
Mass	$100\pi\rho$	$49\pi\rho$	$51\pi\rho$
Distance from A to centre of mass	0 mm	3 mm	d

Take moments about A to calculate d

$$M\bar{x} = \Sigma m_i x_i$$

$$100\pi\rho \times 0 = 49\pi\rho \times 3 + 51\pi\rho \times d$$

$$d = -\frac{147}{51} = -2.88 \text{ to 2 d.p.}$$

Notice that π and the density ρ both cancel out.

The centre of mass of the earring lies on the line AB and is 2.88 mm to the left of A.

ii) When suspended from point P, the centre of mass G is directly below the point P.

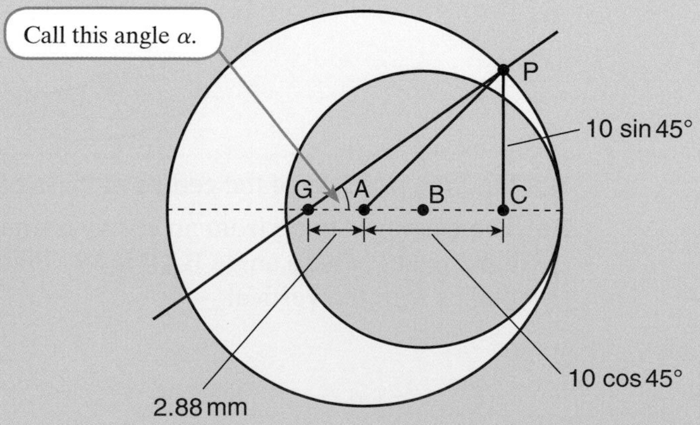

The angle line AB makes with the vertical is the angle PGA. Call this angle α.

In the triangle PGC, $\angle PCG = 90°$.

$GC = GA + AC = 2.88 + 10\cos 45°$

$PC = 10\sin 45°$

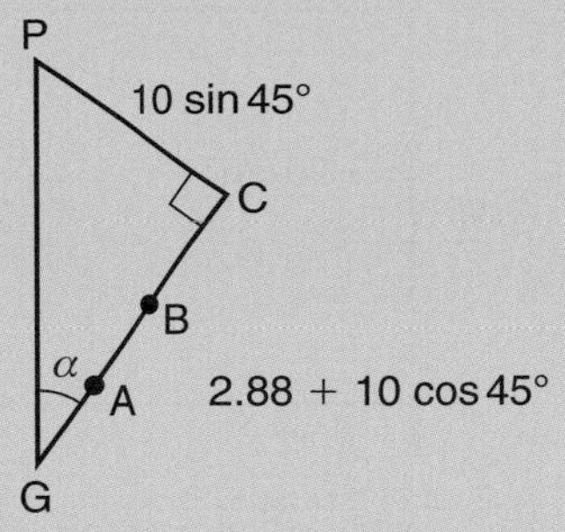

$$\tan\alpha = \frac{10\sin 45°}{2.88 + 10\cos 45°} = 0.71$$

$$\alpha = 35.4°$$

The line AB makes an angle of 35.4° with the vertical.

Test Yourself

1 Four masses are attached to a light framework as shown in the diagram. Find the position of the centre of mass of the framework with reference to the corner labelled O.

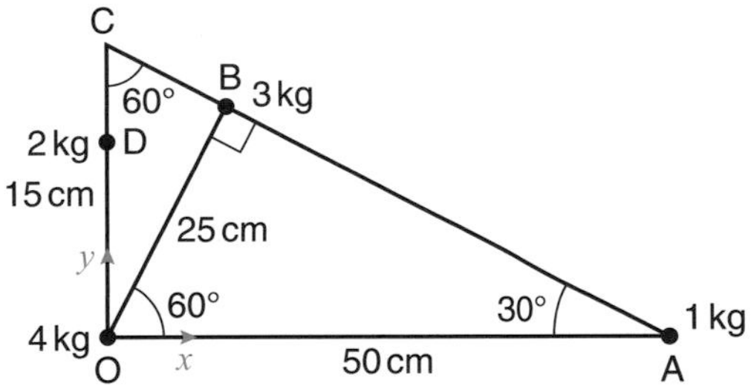

A (14.58, 15.83) **B** (12.5, 10.5) **C** (8.75, 9.50) **D** (11.50, 6.75)

2 The shape in the diagram is cut from a uniform sheet of metal.

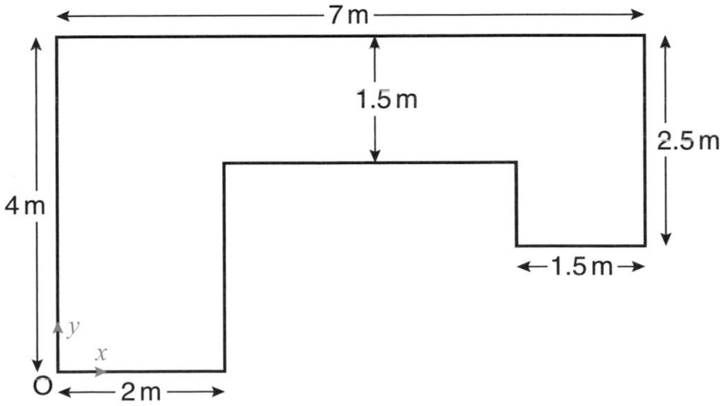

Find the position of the centre of mass from the corner of the plate O. Distances are in metres.

A (3.01, 2.55) **B** (10.75, 6.5) **C** (2.93, 2.55) **D** (3.01, 2.60)

3 A uniform rectangular steel plate, ABCD, has a mass 0.7 kg cut from it, leaving a circular hole. The centre of the hole is 20 cm from AB and 10 cm from BC. The mass of the original plate was 4.2 kg.

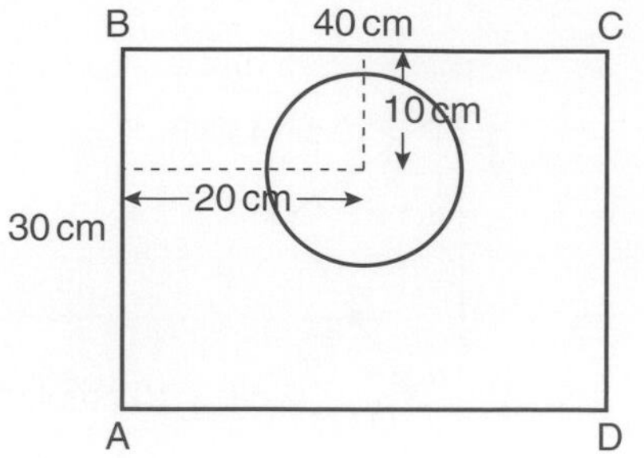

Find the distance of the centre of mass from the edge AD.

A 20 cm **B** 14 cm **C** 22 cm **D** 16 cm

4 A uniform, thin, heavy square plate, OPQR, has sides of length of 50 cm and its mass is 5 kg. Two balls are hung from corners O and Q using light strings. The ball at corner O has mass 2 kg and its centre is 15 cm below the plate. The ball at corner Q has mass 3 kg and its centre is 25 cm below the plate.

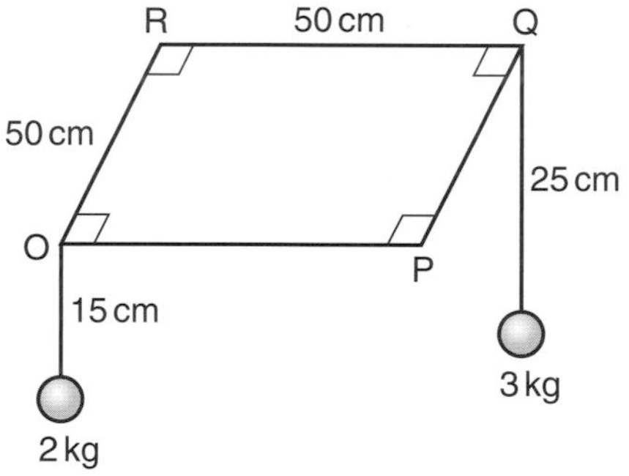

The plate lies in a horizontal plane.

Find the x, y and z co-ordinates of the centre of mass of the whole object using corner O as the origin, OP as the x axis, OR as the y axis and the upwards vertical as the z axis. Distances are in centimetres.

A $(30, 30, -21)$ **B** $(27.5, 27.5, -7.5)$

C $(27.5, 27.5, 10.5)$ **D** $(27.5, 27.5, -10.5)$

Exam-Style Question

K&A Narrowboats lets out boats for holidays on the Kennet and Avon Canal in Wiltshire. The company's office has a sign, in the shape of a narrowboat, hanging outside.

The density of the material from which the sign is made is $2\,\text{g}\,\text{cm}^{-2}$. The sign is modelled as a uniform lamina with three parts: a rectangle OPRW, a rectangle VSTU with a rectangular hole 10 cm by 40 cm and a triangle PQR, as shown in the following diagram. The window is positioned symmetrically within the rectangle.

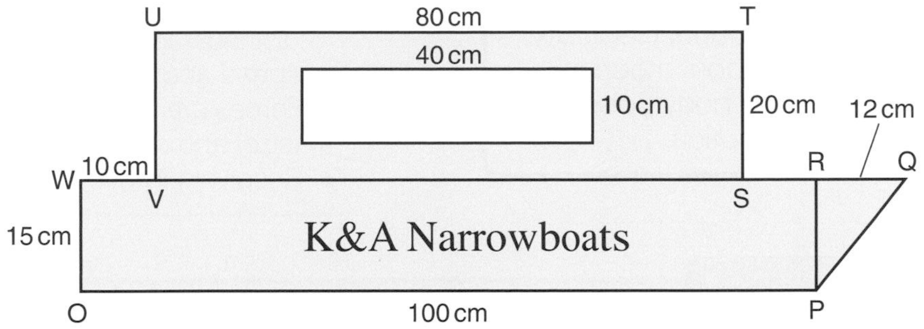

You are given that the centre of mass of the triangle PQR is 4 cm from PR and 5 cm from RQ.

i) Find the mass and centre of mass of each of these three parts referred to x and y axes along OP and OW.

ii) Find the position of the centre of mass of the sign.

The sign is normally suspended from supports at U and T so that UT is horizontal. However, the fixing at T has broken and the sign hangs in equilibrium from the point U.

iii) Find the acute angle that UT makes with the vertical. Give your answer in degrees, correct to one decimal place.

5 Energy, work and power

87
88, 96
101, 109

Energy

A ABOUT THIS TOPIC

In everyday life you are familiar with energy in the forms of heat, light, sound, electricity and so on. This section is about mechanical energy, that is, the energy a body possesses because of its position or motion.

R REMEMBER

- The meanings of position, displacement, distance, velocity, speed and acceleration from M1.
- Forces are vectors with magnitude (size) and direction from M1.
- Resolving forces from M1.

K KEY FACTS

- The work done by a constant force is defined as Fs when F is the force doing the work and s is the distance moved **in the direction of the force**.
- When a force does work on a body it changes the energy of the body.
- The kinetic energy of a body is the energy it possesses because of its motion and is given by $\frac{1}{2}mv^2$ where m is the mass of the body and v its velocity.
- The potential energy of a body is the energy it possesses because of its position.
- The gravitational potential energy of a body is the energy it possesses because of its height and is given by mgh where h is the height of the body above a given level. The reference level for the height is arbitrary and needs to be specified.
- The work–energy principle states that the total work done on a body by all the external forces acting on it is equal to the increase in kinetic energy of the body.
- In any situation energy is conserved, but where there is motion against friction some of this will be in the form of heat.
- The S.I. unit for work is the joule. This is also the unit for energy.

Work

The work done by a constant force F acting over a distance s in the direction of the force is given by Fs. The S.I. unit for work and for energy is the joule.

Kinetic energy

The energy a body possesses because of its motion is called its kinetic energy (K.E.), and is given by $\frac{1}{2}mv^2$.

The first example shows that bodies of very different masses can have the same kinetic energy.

EXAMPLE 1

Find the kinetic energy of each of the objects described below.

i) A small rock of mass 4 kg travelling at $10\,000\ \mathrm{m\,s^{-1}}$ through space.

ii) A train of mass 160 tonnes moving at $50\ \mathrm{m\,s^{-1}}$.

SOLUTION

i) $\text{K.E.} = \frac{1}{2} \times 4 \times (10\,000)^2$
$= 2 \times 100\,000\,000$
$= 2 \times 10^8\ \text{J}$

Remember
1 tonne = 1000 kg

ii) $\text{K.E.} = \frac{1}{2} \times 160\,000 \times (50)^2$
$= 80\,000 \times 2500$
$= 200\,000\,000$
$= 2 \times 10^8\ \text{J}$

Potential energy

The energy a body possesses because of its position is called its potential energy.

The usual formula for gravitational potential energy is mgh. The next example shows you how this arises, starting with the work done in raising a body.

EXAMPLE 2

Find the work done when a body of mass 4 kg is raised at constant speed vertically by 5 m.

Hence write down the increase in potential energy of the body.

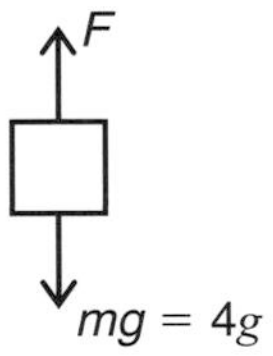

SOLUTION

In this situation a constant force F is being applied and, since there is no acceleration, $F = mg$.

In this example the force $F = mg$ and the distance $s = h$, the height the body is raised, giving the familiar formula mgh.

The work done by the force $= F \times s$
$= 4g \times 5$
$= 20g$
$= 196\ \text{J}$

If the body had been lowered then there would have been a decrease in potential energy and the answer would have been negative.

Increase in potential energy of the body = 196 J.

This is an increase in potential energy because the body has been raised above its initial level.

The next example shows how the work done by a force depends on the angle at which the force is applied.

EXAMPLE 3

A box of mass 5 kg is at rest on a horizontal table. A force of 100 N is applied at 60° to the horizontal. This moves the box a distance of 3 m along the table. It is then again at rest. Find the work done by the force.

SOLUTION

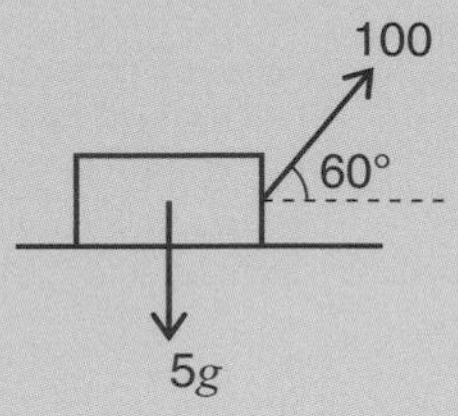

Only the horizontal component of the force does work in this case. The vertical component is at right angles to the direction of motion and so does not contribute to the work.

$$\begin{aligned}\text{Work done} &= 100\cos 60^\circ \times 3\\ &= 100 \times 0.5 \times 3\\ &= 150\,\text{J}\end{aligned}$$

The next example shows how the work-energy principle is used; this states that the total work done on a body by all the external forces acting on it is equal to the increase in its kinetic energy.

EXAMPLE 4

A car of mass 1200 kg is travelling along a straight horizontal road. It accelerates uniformly from 12 m s^{-1} to 18 m s^{-1} in a distance of 200 m. The driving force of the car is 800 N. Find the resistance to motion.

SOLUTION

Let the resistance to motion be R N. So the resultant horizontal force on the car is $(800 - R)$.

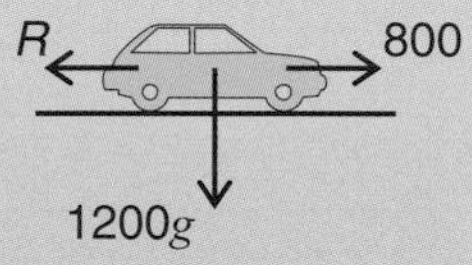

$$\begin{aligned}\text{Gain in K.E.} &= \tfrac{1}{2} \times 1200 \times (18^2 - 12^2)\\ &= 600 \times (324 - 144)\\ &= 600 \times 180\\ &= 108\,000\,\text{J}\end{aligned}$$

$$\begin{aligned}\text{Work done} &= F \times s\\ &= (800 - R) \times 200\end{aligned}$$

Using the work–energy principle,

$$\begin{aligned}\text{Work done} &= \text{increase in K.E.}\\ (800 - R) \times 200 &= 108\,000\\ 160\,000 - 200R &= 108\,000\\ R &= 260\,\text{N}\end{aligned}$$

The next example is similar to the last one but uses conservation of energy as an alternative method to the work-energy principle.

EXAMPLE 5

A car of mass 1100 kg is travelling along a straight horizontal road. Initially its speed is 20 m s^{-1}. The driving force is 2100 N. Resistance forces are constant at 800 N.

i) Find the work done by the car as it travels a further 50 m.

ii) Calculate the work done against the resistances.

iii) Find the speed of the car at the end of the 50 m.

SOLUTION

i) Work done by the car's engine = driving force × distance
$= 2100 \times 50$
$= 105\,000$ J

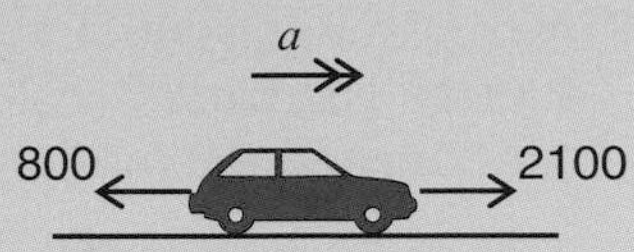

ii) Work done against resistances = 800×50
$= 40\,000$ J

iii) Increase in energy of the car = $105\,000 - 40\,000$
$= 65\,000$ J

Since the road is horizontal this is the increase in the car's kinetic energy.

$$\tfrac{1}{2} \times 1100 \times (v^2 - 20^2) = 65\,000$$
$$1100 \times (v^2 - 400) = 130\,000$$
$$v^2 = 518.1818\ldots$$
$$v = 22.76\ldots$$

The initial K.E. of the car was $\frac{1}{2} \times 1100 \times 20^2$.

The speed is 22.8 m s^{-1} (to 3 s.f.).

In the next example, the work-energy principle is applied in the vertical direction.

EXAMPLE 6

A lift and its occupants have a total mass of 740 kg. As the lift starts to ascend from rest the tension in the cable is 7500 N.

i) Find the work done by the tension as the lift rises 2 m.

ii) Find the increase in potential energy of the lift and hence write down the work done against gravity as the lift rises through 2 m.

iii) What is the speed of the lift when it has risen 2 m?

SOLUTION

i) Work done by the tension in the cable = Fs
$= 7500 \times 2$
$= 15\,000$ J

ii) Increase in P.E. = mgh
$= 740 \times 9.8 \times 2$
$= 14\,504$ J

Work done against gravity = 14 504 J

iii) Total work done = $15\,000 - 14\,504 = 496$ J

Using the work–energy principle

work done = increase in K.E.

$$496 = \tfrac{1}{2} \times 740 \times v^2$$
$$v^2 = 1.3405\ldots$$
$$v = 1.1578\ldots \text{ m s}^{-1}$$

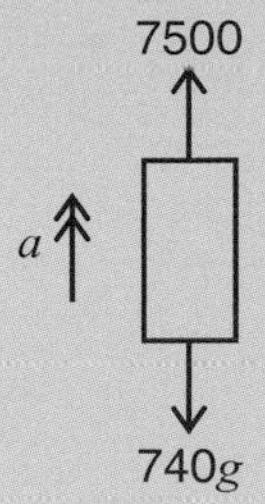

The lift's speed is 1.16 m s^{-1} (to 3 s.f.).

LINKS

Mechanics — Motion in a vertical circle (M3), Elastic strings and springs (M3).

Test Yourself

1 A truck of mass 4000 kg is moving along a straight horizontal road. There is a driving force of 8000 N. The truck accelerates from 0.5 m s^{-1} to 10 m s^{-1} over a distance of 60 m. Work out the resistance to the motion of the truck, assuming it is constant.

A 4675 N **B** 4992 N **C** 3192 N **D** 3325 N

2 A box of weight 12 N is initially at rest. It is pulled a distance of 5 m along a smooth, horizontal floor by a cable inclined at 30° to the upward vertical. The tension in the cable is 28 N. Find the work done by the tension.

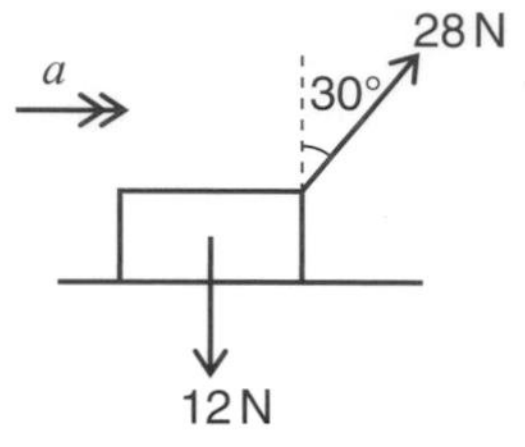

A 121.2 J **B** 140 J **C** 70 J **D** 10 J

3 A crane lifts a load of weight 7350 N vertically into the air. The load is initially at rest. As the load rises the tension in the cable is 7500 N. Find the speed of the load when it has risen 10 m.

A 0.6 m s^{-1} **B** 2 m s^{-1} **C** $10\sqrt{2}$ m s^{-1} **D** 14 m s^{-1}

Exam-Style Question

In a shooting competition, targets are placed directly in front of bags of sand. Each bullet has a mass of 20 g and travels at a speed of 100 m s^{-1}. The bullets penetrate the sand to a depth of 125 cm.

i) Using the work–energy principle, calculate the work done by the sand in stopping a bullet.

ii) Using your answer to **i)**, work out the average force exerted by the sand on a bullet.

iii) The thickness of the sand bags is 2.2 m. Find the maximum speed at which a bullet could be fired and stopped by the sand. Comment briefly on your answer from a safety point of view.

Potential energy

A ABOUT THIS TOPIC

In the previous section you encountered the types of mechanical energy that a body can possess and also how 'work' is defined. In this section you will find out how these ideas can help solve problems involving forces, work and energy.

R REMEMBER

- Definitions of kinetic energy (K.E.), potential energy (P.E.) and work done from M2.

K KEY FACTS

- When an object of mass m is raised through a height h, work is done against gravity and this is stored as gravitational potential energy, mgh.
- When an object is at a point above a given level and is then released, it will lose gravitational potential energy as it falls and gain kinetic energy, $\frac{1}{2}mv^2$.
- If all of the gravitational potential energy lost in the fall is converted to kinetic energy, the system is said to be conservative.
- A system where no external force except gravity operates is conservative and for such a system K.E. + P.E. = constant.
- The work done by a constant force F acting over a distance s in the direction of the force is Fs.
- When the total mechanical energy of a system is changed by the action of the external forces then the system is non-conservative and
initial mechanical energy (K.E. + P.E.) + work done by external forces = final mechanical energy.
- A resistance force acts against the motion and so the force and the work done are often treated as negative.

A lot of problems can be solved either by using Newton's laws or by energy methods. Where you have a choice, use energy if you can as it is often simpler.

> ⚠ When you are using gravitational potential energy always remember to define the reference level.

This example shows how defining the reference level influences your working.

EXAMPLE 1

A ball of mass 0.5 kg is thrown vertically upwards with a speed of 3.5 m s^{-1}. Assuming resistance forces are negligible, find its speed when it is 5 m below its starting point. Take the P.E. to be zero at the point of projection.

SOLUTION

At the start
P.E. = 0
K.E. = $\frac{1}{2} \times 0.5 \times (3.5)^2 = 3.0625$ J
Total energy = 3.0625 J

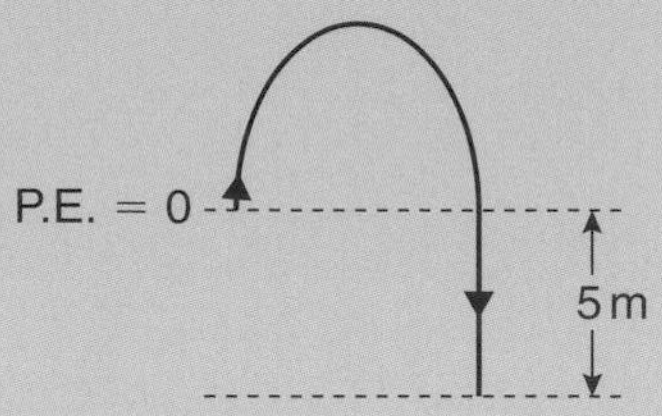

When it has fallen 5 metres
P.E. = $0.5 \times 9.8 \times (-5) = -24.5$ J
K.E. = $\frac{1}{2}mv^2 = 0.25v^2$
Total energy = $-24.5 + 0.25v^2$

Using conservation of mechanical energy
$-24.5 + 0.25v^2 = 3.0625$
$\Rightarrow v = 10.5$
Its speed is 10.5 m s^{-1}.

In the next example you will see how using the information in the question to set the reference level of P.E. helps you understand what is happening.

EXAMPLE 2

A stone of mass 0.4 kg is catapulted vertically upwards from point A with a speed of 21 m s^{-1}. Find the height, h, of the stone relative to A when the speed is

i) 4.2 m s^{-1} **ii)** 35 m s^{-1}.

Assume resistance forces are negligible.

SOLUTION

Take the reference level for P.E. to be at A.

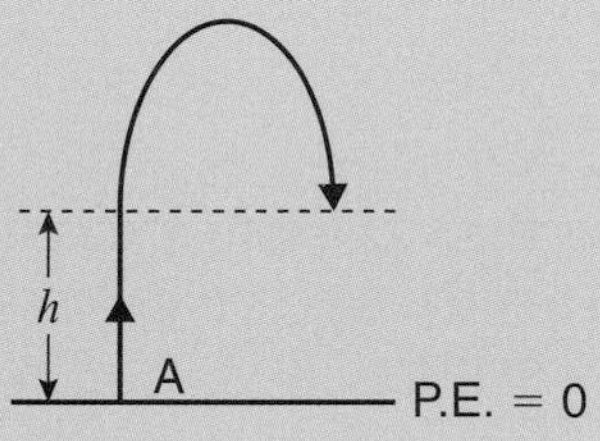

i) At A, P.E. = 0
K.E. = $\frac{1}{2} \times 0.4 \times 21^2 = 88.2$ J
When $v = 4.2$ m s^{-1}
K.E. = $\frac{1}{2} \times 0.4 \times (4.2)^2 = 3.528$ J
Loss in K.E. = 84.672 J
Gain in P.E. = $0.4 \times 9.8 \times h = 3.92h$ J
Using conservation of energy
$3.92h = 84.672 \Rightarrow h = 21.6$
The stone is at a height of 21.6 m above A.

This could be when the stone is on the way up or when it is on the way down.

ii) When the speed is 35 m s^{-1} the stone has gained K.E., so it must have lost P.E. and hence be below A.
When $v = 35$ K.E. = $\frac{1}{2} \times 0.4 \times 35^2 = 245$ J
Gain in K.E. = $245 - 88.2 = 156.8$ J
Gain in P.E. = $0.4 \times 9.8 \times h = 3.92h$ J

You already know the K.E. at A is 88.2 J from part **i)**.

Using conservation of energy
$3.92h + 156.8 = 0 \Rightarrow h = -40$
The stone is 40 m below A.

Note: The negative sign means the stone is below A.

In the next example you don't know the shape of the track that is being followed and so you cannot use Newton's laws. You must use the principle of conservation of energy.

EXAMPLE 3

A sledge has mass 160 kg. Initially it is moving at $1\,\mathrm{m\,s^{-1}}$ at a point 10 m above the lowest point of a track. Assuming air resistance and friction to be negligible, find the speed of the sledge at its lowest point.

SOLUTION

Take the level of the lowest point to be the reference level for potential energy.

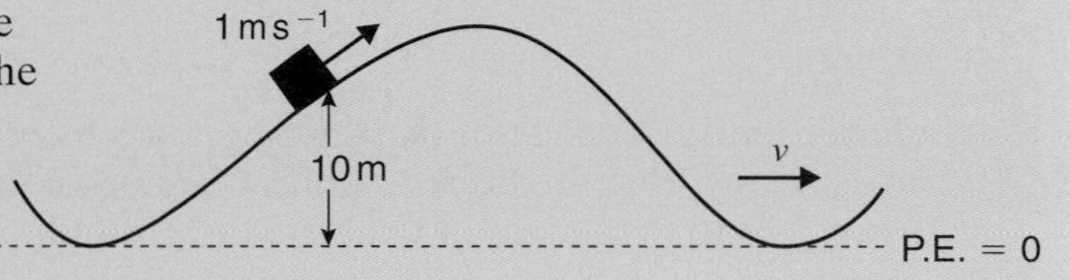

Initially
P.E. $= 160 \times 9.8 \times 10 = 15\,680$ J
K.E. $= \frac{1}{2} \times 160 \times 1^2 = 80$ J

At the lowest point
P.E. $= 0$
K.E. $= \frac{1}{2} \times 160 \times v^2$

Note: The route of the sledge between its starting point and the lowest point does not need to be known in this case as the system is conservative.

Using conservation of energy
$15\,680 + 80 = \frac{1}{2} \times 160 \times v^2$
$v = 14.035\ldots\,\mathrm{m\,s^{-1}}$

The speed of the sledge is $14.0\,\mathrm{m\,s^{-1}}$ (to 3 s.f.)

The next example shows how to solve a problem involving systems that are not conservative.

EXAMPLE 4

A cyclist freewheels down a hill. At the top of the hill his speed is $2\,\mathrm{m\,s^{-1}}$ and at the bottom of the hill it is $10\,\mathrm{m\,s^{-1}}$. The total mass of the cyclist and his machine is 90 kg and the total work done against resistance forces is 8910 J. Find the difference in height between the bottom and the top of the hill.

SOLUTION

Take the reference level for potential energy to be at the bottom of the hill.

At the top of the hill:
P.E. $= 90 \times 9.8 \times h = 882h$ J
K.E. $= \frac{1}{2} \times 90 \times 2^2 = 180$ J
Total mechanical energy $= 882h + 180$ J

At the bottom of the hill:
P.E. $= 0$
K.E. $= \frac{1}{2} \times 90 \times 10^2 = 4500$ J

Total mechanical energy $= 4500$ J
Work done by resistance forces $= (-)8910$ J

Another way of saying this is 'Work done against resistance = 8910 J'.

Using conservation of energy
$882h + 180 - 8910 = 4500$
$882h = 13\,230 \Rightarrow h = 15$

The difference in level between the bottom and the top of the hill is 15 m.

LINKS

Mechanics — Elasticity (M3), Oscillations (M3), Stability of Equilibrium (M4).

Test Yourself

1 A tile of mass 3 kg falls vertically from the edge of a roof to the ground 6 m below. Its speed is $1\,\text{m s}^{-1}$ when it leaves the roof. Air resistance is constant at 20 N during the fall. Find the speed at which the tile hits the ground, to 1 d.p.

A $10.9\,\text{m s}^{-1}$ **B** $6.2\,\text{m s}^{-1}$ **C** $14.1\,\text{m s}^{-1}$ **D** $6.1\,\text{m s}^{-1}$

2 In a fairground ride, a car of mass 500 kg starts from rest at point P which is 30 m above the ground. It travels 73 m along the track to point Q against constant resistances of 600 N. At Q it is travelling at $16\,\text{m s}^{-1}$. Find the height of Q above the ground.

A 8 m **B** 16.8 m **C** 22 m **D** 34.1 m

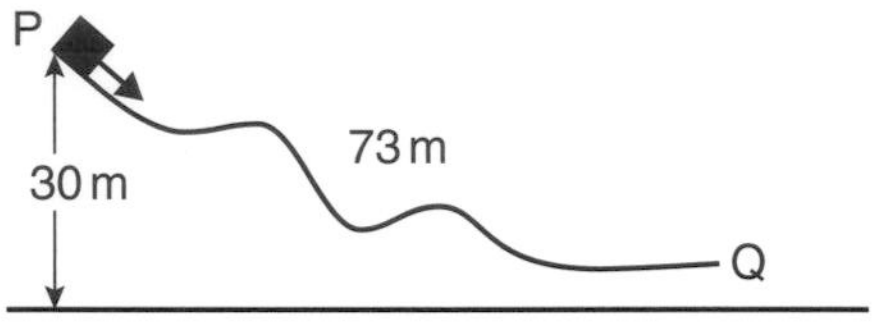

3 A skydiver steps out of a stationary helicopter at a height of 700 m. He freefalls for 500 m, attaining a speed of $30\,\text{m s}^{-1}$ downwards. He then opens his parachute and is travelling at $6\,\text{m s}^{-1}$ when he reaches the ground. The mass of the skydiver and his equipment is 80 kg.

Three of the following statements are false and one is true. Which is the true statement?

A If the skydiver had not opened his parachute he would have been travelling at $42\,\text{m s}^{-1}$ when he reached the ground.

B The skydiver had gained 1440 J of mechanical energy just before he hit the ground.

C During the second part of the descent, air resistance does 155 360 J of work.

D During the complete descent, the skydiver loses 548 800 J of gravitational potential energy.

Exam-Style Question

The diagram shows part of a roller coaster ride. The loop is a circle; its diameter, BC, is 6 m. The point A is 12 m higher than B. The car and its riders have a mass of 260 kg and the car is momentarily at rest at A. On the section ABCB you may assume resistance forces are negligible.

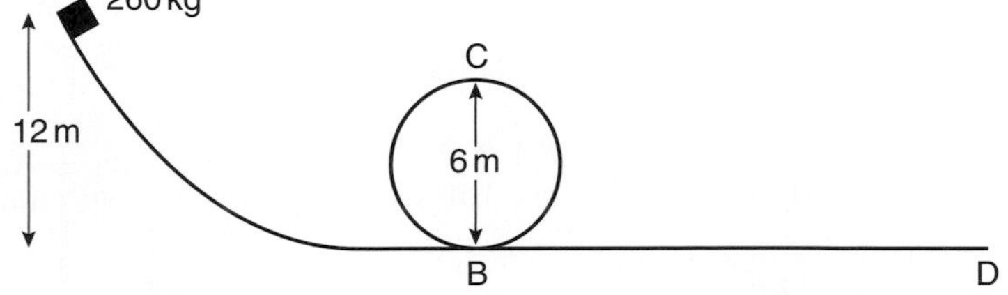

i) Find the kinetic energy of the car when it first reaches B and hence find its speed at this time.

ii) Calculate the speed of the car when it reaches C at the top of the loop.

iii) How would the results compare if the mass of the car and its riders was 300 kg?

BD is a rough horizontal section of track, 50 m long. The car comes to rest at D.

iv) Calculate the average resistance to motion on this section of the track.

Work in two-dimensional motion

A ABOUT THIS TOPIC

In this section, the ideas of work and energy developed in the last two sections are now applied to solve more complex problems and in particular to problems involving motion in two dimensions.

R REMEMBER

- Kinematics and Newton's laws of motion from M1.
- Motion in two dimensions from M1.
- Friction from M2.
- Work from M2.
- Kinetic and potential energy from M2.

K KEY FACTS

- The **work done** by a constant force is the product of the force and the distance moved in the direction of the force.
  - If the force F, and the distance moved s, are in the same direction then the work done $= Fs$.
  - If the direction of the distance moved, s, is at an angle θ to the direction of the force, F, then the work done $= Fs\cos\theta$.
  - The S.I. unit of work is the joule (J).
- The **energy** of a body is its capacity for doing work. The S.I. unit of energy is the joule (J).
- The **work–energy principle** states that the total work done by all the forces acting on a body is equal to the increase in the kinetic energy of the body.
- **Mechanical energy**, which is the sum of the kinetic energy and gravitational potential energy, is conserved when no forces other than gravity do work.

⚠ Both work and energy are scalar quantities.

EXAMPLE 1

A girl pulls a 50 kg sledge 10 m across ice using a rope inclined at 20° to the horizontal. The tension in the rope is 150 N. What is the work done by the girl?

SOLUTION

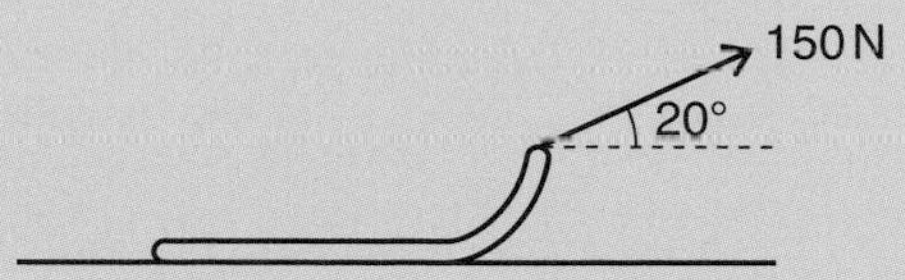

The distance moved in the direction of the force is $(10\cos 20°)$ m.

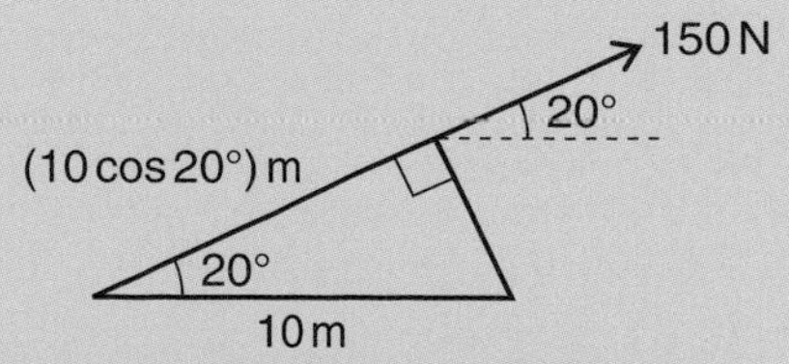

You could have quoted the result work done $= Fs\cos\theta$.

So the work done $= 150 \times (10\cos 20°) = 1410$ J.

An alternative approach is as follows:

SOLUTION

The basic definition of **work done** by a constant force is 'the product of the force and the distance moved in the direction of the force', which gives the formula

$$\text{work done} = Fs\cos\theta$$

This can be written as $(F\cos\theta) \times s$ and interpreted as (the component of F in the direction of the distance moved) $\times$ (distance moved).

This is $150\cos 20° \times 10$ or 1410 J, as before.

The two solutions show that sometimes it is helpful to take the component of the force in the direction of the distance rather than the component of the distance in the direction of the force. Both approaches are correct and equally valid.

EXAMPLE 2

A string of length 1.2 m is attached to a fixed point and has a small object of mass 0.5 kg at its other end. Initially the object is held with the string, which is kept taut, making an angle of 40° with the vertical. It is released to swing freely as a pendulum. What is its speed when it passes through the lowest point of its path?

SOLUTION

Start by drawing a diagram showing the path of the pendulum and then set up the model:

- Take the reference level for P.E. to be the lowest point.
- Let the speed of the body at B be $v\,\text{m s}^{-1}$.

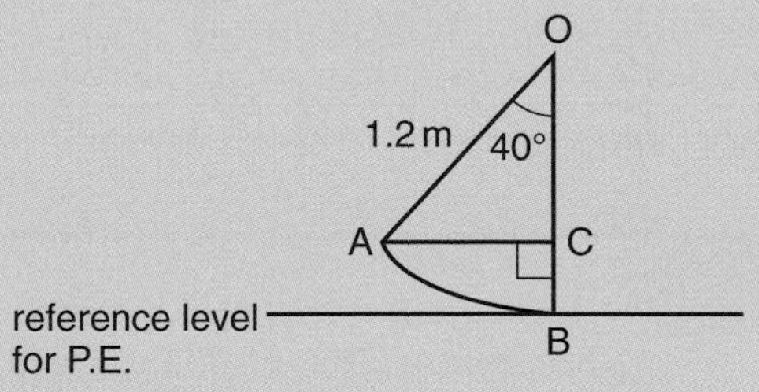

See Key facts.

As there are no forces other than gravity, mechanical energy is conserved.

At A: P.E. $= mgh = 0.5 \times 9.8 \times 1.2\,(1 - \cos 40°)$
$= 1.375\ldots$

K.E. $= 0$ — Initially the object is at rest.

BC = OB − OC = 1.2 − 1.2 cos 40°

So the total mechanical energy $= 1.375\ldots + 0 = 1.375\ldots$ J — = P.E. + K.E.

At B: P.E. $= 0$ — P.E. = 0 as $h = 0$.

K.E. $= \frac{1}{2} \times 0.5 \times v^2 = 0.25v^2$

So the total mechanical energy $= 0 + 0.25v^2 = 0.25v^2$ J

Using conservation of energy $0.25v^2 = 1.375\ldots$

$\therefore v = 2.345\ldots$

The speed of the object at B is $2.35\,\text{m s}^{-1}$ (to 3 s.f.).

This result does not depend on the mass at the end of the string. In this question the mass is 0.5 kg. It cancels out in the equation above.

EXAMPLE 3

A body of mass 3 kg is projected with a speed of $15\,\mathrm{m\,s^{-1}}$ up a rough slope which is inclined at 20° to the horizontal. Assume that friction is the only resisting force acting on the body and that the coefficient of friction is μ. The body comes to rest after travelling 25 m up the slope.

i) How much energy has been lost to friction?

ii) Find the value of the coefficient of friction μ.

SOLUTION

i) This diagram illustrates the important information.

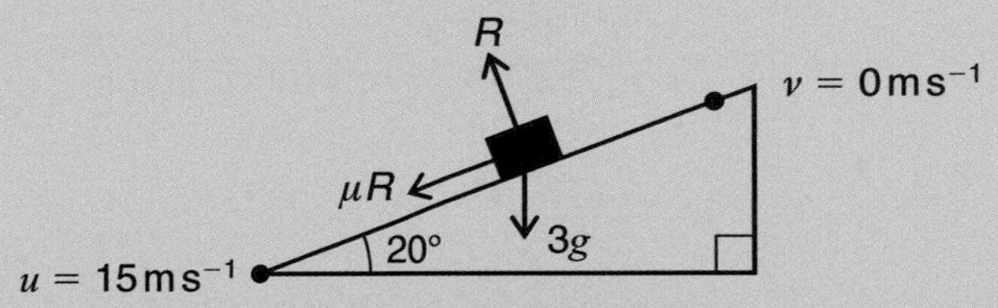

There are three forces acting on the body.
Let W be the work done by the frictional force.

Force	**Work**
Force of gravity, $3g$	$-3g \times (25 \sin 20°)$
Frictional force	W
Normal reaction, R	0

This is the energy which has been lost to friction and so is what the question asks you to find.

As the normal reaction is perpendicular to the direction of motion.

The total work done by all the forces $= W - 3g \times (25 \sin 20°)$
$= W - 251.3848\ldots$

The increase in kinetic energy $= 0 - \frac{1}{2} \times 3 \times 15^2 = -337.5$

Using the work–energy principle $W - 251.3848\ldots = -337.5$

$\therefore \quad W = -86.115\ldots$

So the work done by friction is $-86.115\ldots$ J.

This means that 86.1 J has been lost to friction.

ii) The question now asks for the value of the coefficient of friction.

From the diagram, the frictional force is μR, where R is the normal reaction.

Considering the forces perpendicular to the slope gives
$R = 3g \cos 20° = 27.626\ldots$
giving a frictional force of $\mu \times 27.626\ldots$ down the slope.

So the work done by the frictional force is
$(\mu \times -27.626\ldots) \times 25 = -690.674\ldots \times \mu$ (be careful with the signs).

$\therefore \mu \times -690.674\ldots = -86.115\ldots \Rightarrow \mu = 0.12468\ldots$

This is the distance travelled.

The coefficient of friction is 0.125.

EXAMPLE 4

A stone of mass 0.4 kg starts from rest at A and slides down the line of greatest slope of an icy hill AB. The length of the hill is 50 m and the vertical drop from A to B is 10 m.

i) Using the simplified model in which friction and air resistance are ignored, what would be the speed of the stone when it reaches B?

ii) If the stone had only attained a speed of $9\,\mathrm{m\,s^{-1}}$ when it reached B, what resisting force, assumed constant, would have been acting?

SOLUTION

i) Start by drawing a diagram showing the path of the stone and then set up the model.

- OB is the reference level for P.E.
- The speed of the body at B is $v\,\mathrm{m\,s^{-1}}$.

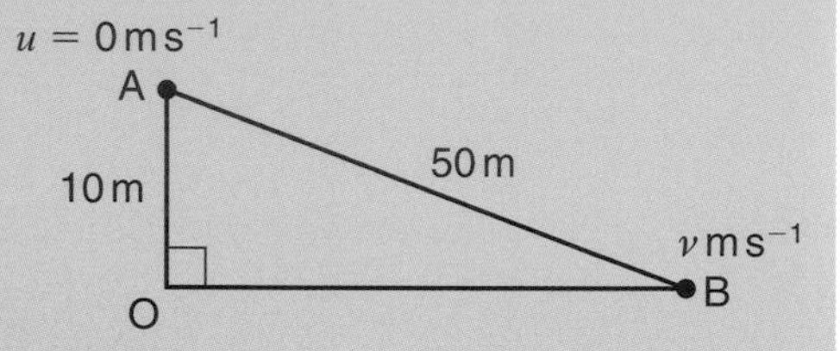

As there are no forces other than gravity, mechanical energy is conserved. ← See Key facts.

At A: P.E. $= 0.4 \times g \times 10 = 39.2$

K.E. $= 0$ ← Initial speed = 0, so K.E. = 0.

So mechanical energy $= 39.2$ J

At B: P.E. $= 0$ ← P.E. = 0 as $h = 0$.

K.E. $= \frac{1}{2} \times 0.4 \times v^2 = 0.2v^2$

So mechanical energy $= 0.2v^2$ ← Mechanical energy is conserved.

$\therefore \quad 39.2 = 0.2v^2 \Rightarrow v = 14\,\mathrm{m\,s^{-1}}$

Therefore the speed when the stone reaches B is $14\,\mathrm{m\,s^{-1}}$.

ii) In this part the work–energy principle applies. ← See Key facts.

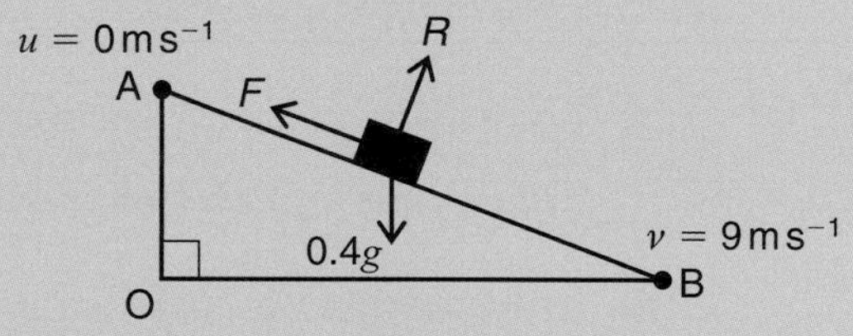

Force	Work
Force of gravity, $0.4g$	$0.4g \times 10 = 39.2$
Resisting force, F	$-50F$ (resisting force is up the slope)
Normal reaction, R	0 ← The normal reaction is perpendicular to the direction of motion.

The total work done by all the forces is $39.2 - 50F$ and the increase in K.E. $= \frac{1}{2} \times 0.4 \times 9^2 - 0 = 16.2$

So $39.2 - 50F = 16.2$

$\Rightarrow \quad 50F = 39.2 - 16.2$

$\Rightarrow \quad F = 0.46$ N

The resisting force is 0.46 N up the slope.

LINKS

Mechanics — Circular motion and Hooke's Law (M3), Variable forces (M4). Modelling with differential equations (DE).

Test Yourself

1 The speed of a tile as it slides off the roof of a house is $5\,\text{m}\,\text{s}^{-1}$. The edge of the roof is 8 m above ground level and the angle of the roof is 45°. Three of the following statements are false and one is true. Which one is true?

A If the angle of the roof were more than 45° to the horizontal, the speed of the tile would be greater when it hits the ground.

B The mechanical energy of the tile increases as it falls.

C The speed of the tile as it hits the ground is $13.5\,\text{m}\,\text{s}^{-1}$.

D The speed of the tile as it leaves the roof is $\begin{pmatrix} \frac{5\sqrt{2}}{2} \\ \frac{-5\sqrt{2}}{2} \end{pmatrix} \text{m}\,\text{s}^{-1}$.

2 The position vector (in metres) of a cricket ball, of mass 150 g, t seconds after it is hit in the air from ground level is modelled by $\mathbf{r} = 20t\,\mathbf{i} + (20t - 5t^2)\,\mathbf{j}$, where the unit vectors $\mathbf{i}$ and $\mathbf{j}$ are in the horizontal and vertical directions. What are the values of the gravitational potential energy and the kinetic energy of the ball when $t = 1.5$? The reference level for P.E. is ground level.

A P.E.= 44.1 J; K.E.= 31.9 J **B** P.E.= 44.1 J; K.E.= 1.88 J

C P.E.= 27.6 J; K.E.= 1.88 J **D** P.E.= 27.6 J; K.E.= 31.9 J

3 An army hut has the shape of half a cylinder of radius 5 m. The roof of the hut reaches the ground at both sides. A vertical cross-section of the hut is shown in the diagram. A box of mass 6 kg is pulled over the roof of the hut, starting from rest at ground level. There is a constant force of 30 N resisting motion and the speed of the box at the top is $2\,\text{m}\,\text{s}^{-1}$. Find the total work done in moving the box from ground level to the highest point of the roof.

A 518 J **B** 542 J

C 248 J **D** 530 J

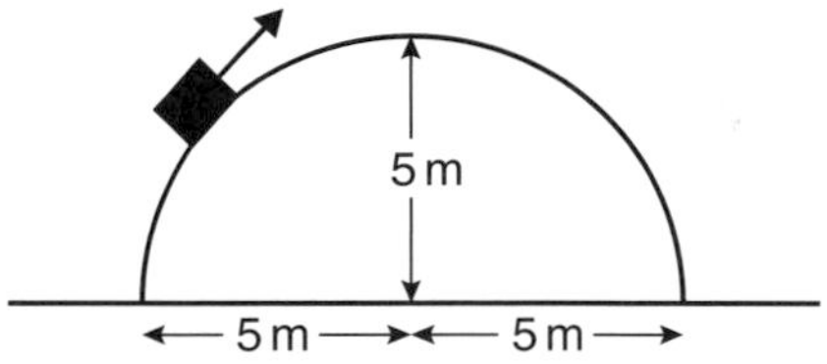

Exam-Style Question

A skier, whose mass is 80 kg, starts from rest at the top of the approach to a ski-jump. The approach is 30 m long and the difference in height between the starting and take-off points is 10 m. He then lands in snow 15 m below his take-off point.

i) A simplified model assumes that there are no forces resisting motion either on the approach or through the air to his landing point. What is his speed as he lands?

ii) In a more refined model, resisting forces of 50 N, while he is on the approach, are included, but still no resisting forces between the take-off point and his landing. With this model, what is his speed as he lands?

iii) Resisting forces while the skier is in the air are now included in the model. The skier covers 30.6 m while he is in the air and his landing speed is $19.8\,\text{m}\,\text{s}^{-1}$. Calculate the average resistance force opposing the motion.

Power

A ABOUT THIS TOPIC

Two machines produce the same amount of work but one takes twice as long as the other. Which machine would you prefer? The rate at which work is being done is an important measure. It is known as *power*.

R REMEMBER

- Kinematics from M1.
- Newton's laws of motion from M1.
- Energy from M2.
- Work from M2.

K KEY FACTS

- Power, P = rate of doing work
  $= \dfrac{\text{work done}}{\text{time taken}}$
- When the power is constant: work done = power × time taken.
- An alternative expression for power is: $P = Fv$
- When the force and velocity are not constant, this relation gives the power produced at the instant when the force is F and the velocity is v.
- The S.I. unit of power is the watt (W); 1 kilowatt (kW) = 1000 W.

EXAMPLE 1

A car maintains a constant speed of $40\,\text{m s}^{-1}$ on a horizontal road. The resistance to motion is 500 N. What power is the engine producing?

SOLUTION

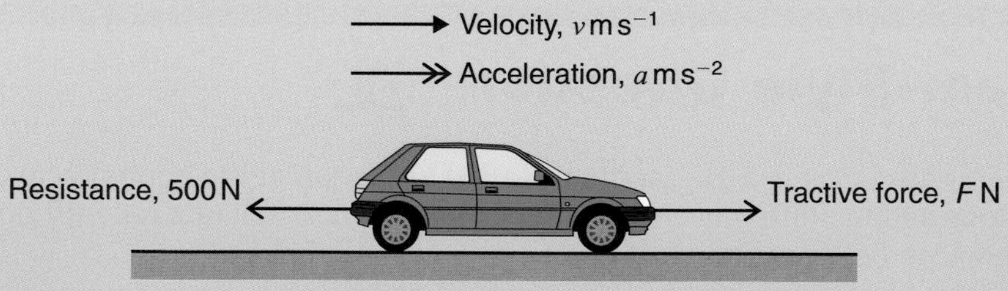

As the car maintains a constant speed, $a = 0$

$$\therefore \quad F - 500 = 0$$
$$\therefore \quad F = 500$$

$$\begin{aligned}\text{Power} &= \text{force} \times \text{velocity}\\ &= 500 \times 40\\ &= 20\,000\end{aligned}$$

Therefore the power the engine is producing is 20 000 W = 20 kW.

EXAMPLE 2

A pump raises water from a reservoir. Each minute it raises 600 kg through 5 m and discharges it at $10\,\text{m}\,\text{s}^{-1}$. What power is the pump producing?

SOLUTION

The water gains both potential energy and kinetic energy.

In one minute:

The potential energy gained $= 600 \times g \times 5 = 29\,400\,\text{J}$ ← P.E. $= mgh$

and the kinetic energy gained $= \frac{1}{2} \times 600 \times 10^2 = 30\,000\,\text{J}$ ← K.E. $= \frac{1}{2}mv^2$

So the total energy gained $= 29\,400 + 30\,000$

$= 59\,400\,\text{J}$

This is the work done by the pump in one minute.

$$\text{Power of the pump} = \frac{\text{work done}}{\text{time taken}}$$

$$= \frac{59\,400}{60}$$

Remember the correct units: work in joules and time in seconds.

$$= 990$$

So the power the pump is producing is 990 W.

EXAMPLE 3

A car of mass 1000 kg is driven along a level road against resistances totalling 300 N. The engine is developing power of 7.5 kW. What is the acceleration of the car when its speed is $15\,\text{m}\,\text{s}^{-1}$?

SOLUTION

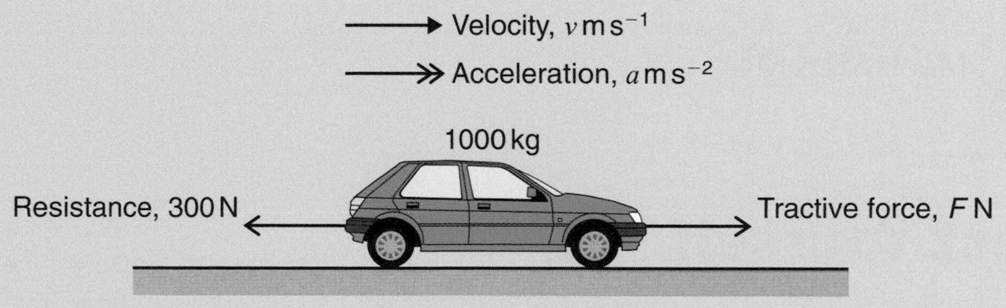

Power $P = Fv$, so substituting for P and v gives

$7500 = F \times 15 \Rightarrow F = 500$

Applying Newton's second law of motion (force = mass × acceleration) gives

$500 - 300 = 1000a$

$\Rightarrow$ the acceleration is $0.2\,\text{m}\,\text{s}^{-2}$.

EXAMPLE 4

A winch, which has a maximum power of 300 W, is used to pull a crate of mass 75 kg against resistances of 150 N. What is the maximum speed of the crate up a slope that is at an angle of 15° to the horizontal?

SOLUTION

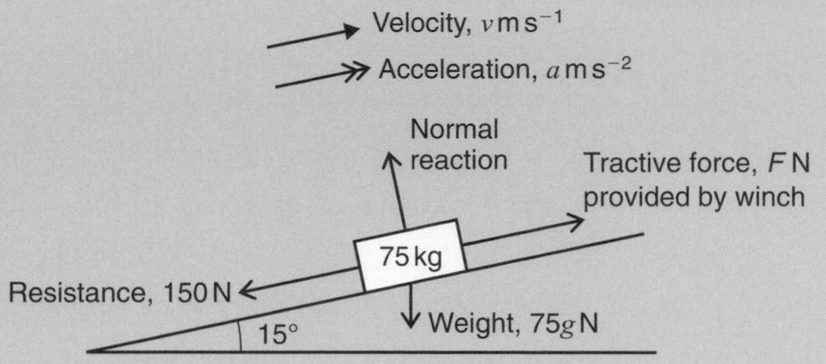

Total force down the slope = resistance + component of weight down the slope

$$= 150 + 75g\sin 15°$$
$$= 340.2$$

At maximum speed, the acceleration = 0,

so the forces up the slope = the forces down the slope,

$\therefore$ The tractive force $F = 340.2$ N

Power $P = Fv$

$\therefore \quad 300 = 340.2v$

$\therefore \quad v = \dfrac{300}{340.2} = 0.88$ (to 2 d.p.)

So the maximum speed of the crate is 0.88 m s^{-1}.

LINKS

Mechanics M4.

Test Yourself

1 A train of mass 40 tonnes is pulled along a level track by a small shunting engine. The resistance to motion is 1200 N. What is the maximum speed of the train when the engine is working at 18 kW?

A 0.03 m s^{-2} **B** 15 m s^{-1} **C** 0.015 m s^{-1} **D** 0.067 m s^{-1}

2 A car of mass 650 kg travels at a constant speed of 8 m s^{-1} up an incline of 5° to the horizontal. The engine is working at the constant rate of 6 kW. What is the magnitude of the resistance to motion? Give your answer correct to 3 significant figures.

A 750 N **B** 693 N **C** 5440 N **D** 195 N

3 A load of 50 tonnes is raised vertically from rest by a crane. The engine of the crane develops a constant power of 9.8×10^4 watts. Three of the following statements are false and one is true. Which one is true? (Ignore any frictional forces and the weight of the cable.)

A When the speed of the load is $0.1\,\mathrm{m\,s^{-1}}$, the tension in the cable is 490 000 N.

B The velocity–time graph of the load looks like this:

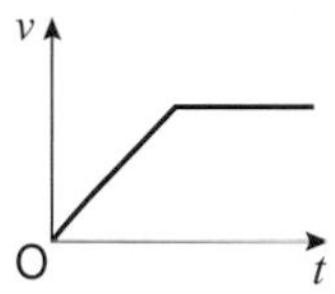

C When the speed of the load is $0.2\,\mathrm{m\,s^{-1}}$, the acceleration is zero.

D When the speed of the load is $0.1\,\mathrm{m\,s^{-1}}$, its acceleration is $0.10\,\mathrm{m\,s^{-2}}$ (to 2 s.f.)

Exam-Style Question

Take $g = 10\,\mathrm{m\,s^{-2}}$ in this question.

A car of mass 800 kg travels along a road ABCD. AB and CD are horizontal and BC is at an angle θ to the horizontal, where $\sin\theta = 0.05$. The distances AB, BC and CD are each 300 m.

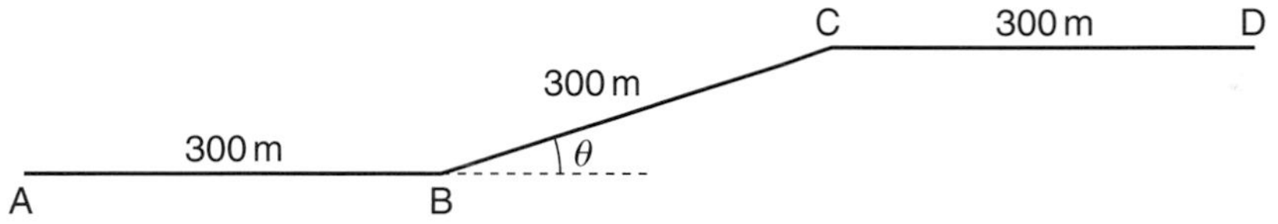

The power developed by the engine remains constant throughout the journey at 30 kW. Assume that the resistance to motion in each of the three sections of the journey is the same and that the car moves smoothly from one section to the next without losing speed.

i) The car has a constant speed of $15\,\mathrm{m\,s^{-1}}$ along AB.

A) Find the resistance to motion.

B) How much work does the engine do while the car travels from A to B?

ii) After the car has passed B it begins to decelerate before reaching a constant speed. Show that this constant speed is $12.5\,\mathrm{m\,s^{-1}}$.

iii) After passing C the car accelerates until it again reaches a constant speed.

A) What is this constant speed?

B) What is the acceleration of the car at C when its speed is $12.5\,\mathrm{m\,s^{-1}}$?

C) Is the acceleration constant during the accelerating phase? Justify your answer.

6 Impulse and momentum

119
128, 138
140, 151

Impulse

A ABOUT THIS TOPIC

Impulse and momentum are both words which have a different meaning in mechanics to that used in everyday English. In sport, we talk about a player acting impulsively or a team gathering momentum to imply that they are unbeatable. In mechanics, however, momentum has a precise meaning and is defined as 'mass × velocity', so a large truck which is moving slowly may have the same momentum as a smaller, fast moving car. When a force acts on an object the momentum of the object changes, such that the longer the force acts for, the greater the change in momentum. This leads to the quantity impulse which is change in momentum or 'average force' × time.

R REMEMBER

- Resolving vectors into perpendicular components from M1.
- Finding the magnitude of a vector from M1.
- Mechanical energy from M2.

K KEY FACTS

- When a constant force acts for a time t, the impulse of the force is defined as:
  impulse = force × time
  The impulse, **J**, is a vector in the direction of the force. Its magnitude is J.
- The S.I. unit for impulse is the newton second (Ns).
- Impulse is also used in situations where the force is not constant.
  In that case
  impulse = average force × time
- The impulse–momentum equation is:
  impulse of force = final momentum − initial momentum
  which can be written as:
  $J = mv - mu$
  or using vector notation as:
  $\mathbf{J} = m\mathbf{v} - m\mathbf{u}$
- The impulse–momentum equation is useful for problems where the force acts for a short time but is not constant, such as in a collision.

Problems on impulse usually involve forces which act for a short length of time such as in a collision. There are two different equations used for impulse – you need to be able to use the right one! Use the impulse–momentum equation if time is not mentioned in the question or if the force is not constant.

EXAMPLE 1

Calculate the impulse required to stop a ball of mass 0.4 kg travelling at $12\,\text{m}\,\text{s}^{-1}$.

SOLUTION

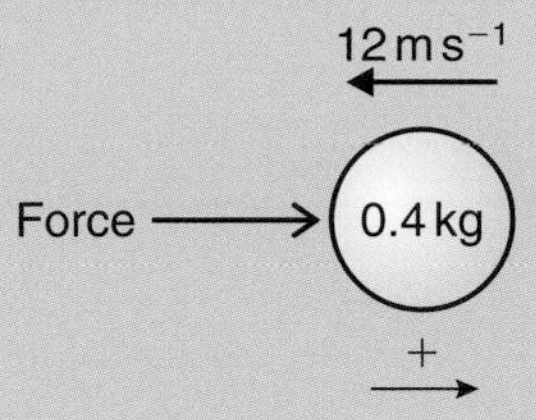

A ADVICE

Always draw a diagram and make it clear which direction you are taking as positive.

Impulse of force = final momentum − initial momentum

$$J = mv - mu$$
$$= 0.4 \times 0 - 0.4 \times (-12)$$
$$= 4.8$$

The ball stops, so its final velocity is 0.

Note this negative velocity. The force is **stopping** the ball, so acts in the **opposite** direction to the ball's motion. In the diagram, the direction of the force has been defined as positive, so the velocity of the ball is negative.

So the impulse required is 4.8 Ns.

A ADVICE

By considering the equation impulse = force × time, you can see that this impulse could have been produced in a number of ways, e.g. by a force of 4.8 N acting for 1 second, by a force of 9.6 N acting for 0.5 second or even by a force of 48 N acting for 0.1 second. Or the force could have varied during the impact.

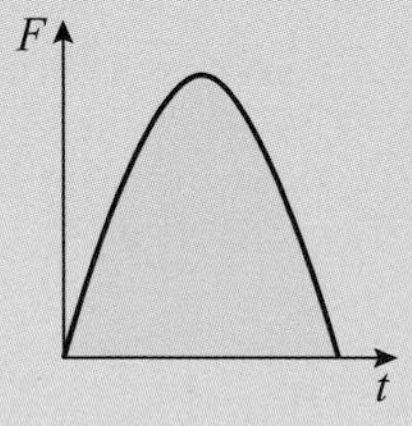

Often the forces involved in an impact are not constant. The impulse can be found from the area under a force–time graph.

When the time that a **constant** force is acting for is given in the question you should use the equation impulse = force × time. You may have to use both equations for impulse within the same question.

Sometimes you may also be asked to work out the change in mechanical energy following an impulse acting on an object.

EXAMPLE 2

Wayne kicks a football, of mass 450 g, at a wall. The ball hits the wall at a speed of $15\,\text{m s}^{-1}$ and then rebounds at a speed of $10\,\text{m s}^{-1}$ along the same horizontal line of action. The ball is in contact with the wall for 0.05 s.

i) Find the average force exerted on the ball.

ii) Find the loss of kinetic energy during the impact.

SOLUTION

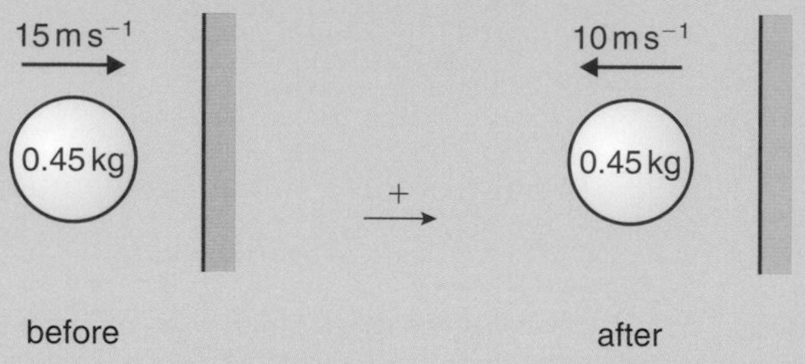

i) Use the impulse–momentum equation to work out the impulse acting on the ball.

$$\begin{aligned} J &= mv - mu \\ &= 0.45 \times (-10) - 0.45 \times 15 \\ &= -11.25\,\text{Ns} \end{aligned}$$

Take care with your signs!

The impulse acts to the 'right' on the wall and to the 'left' on the ball (causing it to rebound). The 'right' direction is positive and so the impulse on the ball (and the force) is negative.

You can now use $J = Ft$ to work out the average force:

$$\begin{aligned} J &= Ft \\ -11.25 &= F \times 0.05 \\ \Rightarrow \quad F &= -225\,\text{N} \end{aligned}$$

So the average force exerted is 225 N. Its direction is away from the wall.

ii) Initial K.E. $= \frac{1}{2} \times 0.45 \times 15^2$
$= 50.625\,\text{J}$

Final K.E. $= \frac{1}{2} \times 0.45 \times 10^2$
$= 22.5\,\text{J}$

K.E. $= \frac{1}{2}mv^2$

Loss in K.E. $= 50.625 - 22.5$
$= 28.1\,\text{J}$ (to 3 s.f.)

Impulse and momentum are both vectors, so you can solve problems that involve more than one dimension. To do this, you should use the equation $\mathbf{J} = m\mathbf{v} - m\mathbf{u}$ and express $\mathbf{J}$, $\mathbf{u}$ and $\mathbf{v}$ either as column vectors or in terms of the unit vectors $\mathbf{i}$ and $\mathbf{j}$.

EXAMPLE 3

In a game of ice hockey, a puck (disc) of mass 160 g is travelling with a speed of $18\,\text{m s}^{-1}$. Jane strikes the puck so it travels at $30\,\text{m s}^{-1}$ at an angle of 60° to its original direction of motion.

Find the magnitude and direction of the impulse exerted on the puck.

SOLUTION

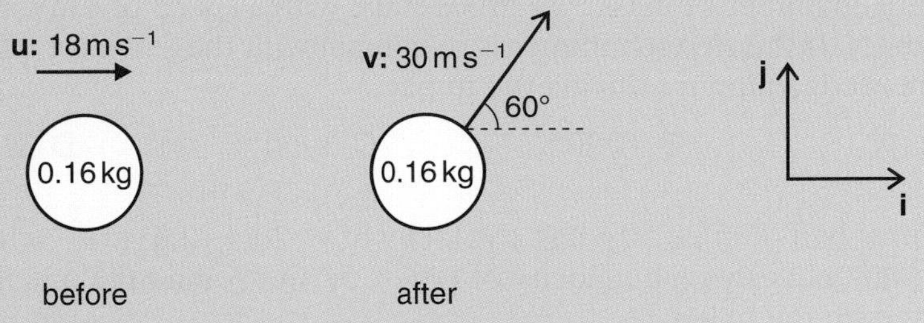

First find **u** and **v** as vectors:

$$\mathbf{u} = \begin{pmatrix}18\\0\end{pmatrix} \text{ and } \mathbf{v} = \begin{pmatrix}30\cos 60^\circ\\30\sin 60^\circ\end{pmatrix} = \begin{pmatrix}15\\15\sqrt{3}\end{pmatrix}$$

You can use $\mathbf{u} = 18\mathbf{i}$ and $\mathbf{v} = 15\mathbf{i} + 15\sqrt{3}\mathbf{j}$ if you prefer.

The impulse exerted on the puck is the change in momentum of the puck:

$$\begin{aligned}\mathbf{J} &= m\mathbf{v} - m\mathbf{u}\\ &= 0.16 \times \begin{pmatrix}15\\15\sqrt{3}\end{pmatrix} - 0.16 \times \begin{pmatrix}18\\0\end{pmatrix}\\ &= \begin{pmatrix}-0.48\\4.156\ldots\end{pmatrix}\end{aligned}$$

Don't round yet, store the number in your calculator.

Draw a diagram to help you find the magnitude and direction of the impulse:

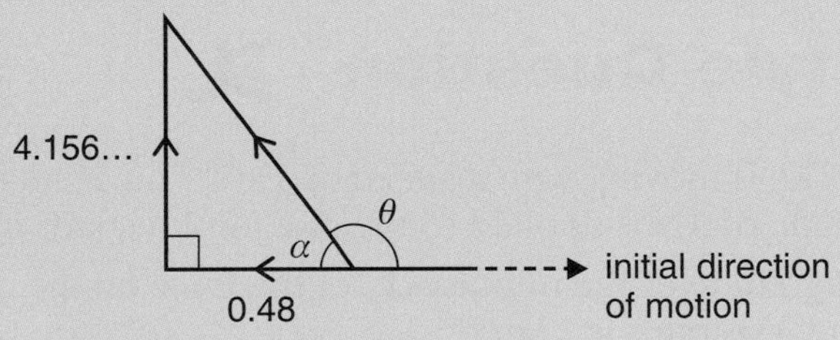

$$\text{Magnitude of the impulse} = \sqrt{0.48^2 + 4.156\ldots^2} = 4.18\,\text{Ns}$$

$$\text{To find the direction: } \tan\alpha = \frac{4.156\ldots}{0.48} = 8.66\ldots$$

$$\alpha = 83.4^\circ$$

$$\theta = 96.6^\circ$$

$\theta = 180^\circ - \alpha$

So the impulse exerted is 4.18 Ns at an angle of 96.6° to the initial direction of travel of the puck.

LINKS

Mechanics — Angular momentum (M4), Variable mass (M4).

Test Yourself

1 Rosie pushes her motorbike with a constant force of magnitude 150 N for 9 seconds. The mass of the motorbike is 300 kg and its speed was originally $0.5\,\text{m s}^{-1}$. Find the motorbike's speed at the end of the 9-second interval. Resistance to motion may be ignored.

A $5\,\text{m s}^{-1}$ **B** $4.5\,\text{m s}^{-1}$ **C** $-5\,\text{m s}^{-1}$ **D** $4\,\text{m s}^{-1}$

2 A sledgehammer of mass 5 kg hits a stake with a speed of $4\,\text{m s}^{-1}$ and then rebounds with a speed of $2\,\text{m s}^{-1}$. If the sledgehammer is in contact with the stake for 0.01 s, find the average force exerted on the sledgehammer during the impact.

A 0.3 N **B** 1000 N **C** 3000 N **D** 30 N

3 A tennis ball of mass 50 g has a velocity of $(-20\mathbf{i} - 25\mathbf{j})\,\text{m s}^{-1}$ when it is hit by a tennis racket. The ball then moves with a velocity of $(40\mathbf{i} + 5\mathbf{j})\,\text{m s}^{-1}$. Find the magnitude and direction of the impulse exerted on the ball.

A $(3\mathbf{i} + 1.5\mathbf{j})$ Ns

B 3350 Ns in a direction of 26.6° to the horizontal

C 3.35 Ns in a direction of 26.6° to the horizontal

D 1.41 Ns in a direction of 45° below the horizontal

4 In a game of marbles, a marble of mass 10 g is travelling with a speed of $5\,\text{m s}^{-1}$ when it is hit by a second marble. After the impact the first marble travels at $2\,\text{m s}^{-1}$ at an angle of 30° to its original direction of motion. Find the magnitude of the impulse exerted on the first marble.

A 0.03 Ns **B** $(-0.013\mathbf{i} + 0.01\mathbf{j})$ Ns **C** 0.026 Ns **D** 0.016 Ns

Exam-Style Question

A disc of mass 2 kg is moving with a speed of $3\,\text{m s}^{-1}$ on a smooth horizontal plane. A force with an average magnitude of 6 N is applied to the disc for 3 seconds along the disc's direction of motion.

i) Find the magnitude of the impulse, $\mathbf{J}_1$, of the force on the disc. Hence show that the speed of the disc after the 3 seconds is $12\,\text{m s}^{-1}$.

Immediately after this 3-second interval, a second impulse, $\mathbf{J}_2$, of 10 Ns at an angle of 60° to the disc's direction of motion is exerted on the disc.

ii) Find the magnitude and direction of the final velocity of the disc.

iii) Show that the overall change in momentum of the disc is equal to $\mathbf{J}_1 + \mathbf{J}_2$.

Conservation of momentum

A ABOUT THIS TOPIC

Momentum is conserved in any closed system; this includes both collisions and situations when bodies separate – this is known as the law of conservation of momentum. You can use this law to help you solve problems which involve situations where bodies either separate (as in an explosion) or collide.

R REMEMBER

- Impulse and momentum from M2.
- Mechanical energy from M2.

K KEY FACTS

- The law of conservation of momentum, also known as the Principle of Conservation of Momentum, states that when no external forces act on a system, the total momentum of the system is constant.

  total momentum **before** = total momentum **after**
- In a collision some mechanical energy is often lost as heat and sound energy.

There are two different types of problem that you may be asked to solve; these are collisions and separations (for example, explosions). The first two examples are on collisions.

A ADVICE

When you solve problems involving conservation of momentum, you should always
- draw a 'before' and 'after' diagram and
- show clearly which direction(s) are positive.

EXAMPLE 1

Two spheres, A of mass 2 kg and B of mass 6 kg, are moving towards each other in the same straight line along a smooth, horizontal plane. Sphere A has a velocity of $5\,\mathrm{m\,s^{-1}}$ and sphere B has velocity $4\,\mathrm{m\,s^{-1}}$. After the collision sphere B moves in the opposite direction with a speed of $2\,\mathrm{m\,s^{-1}}$. Find the velocity of sphere A and the loss in kinetic energy.

SOLUTION

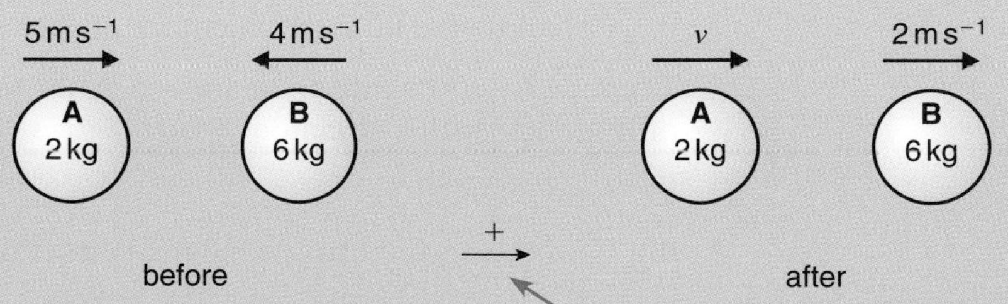

Remember to define the positive direction.

Using the law of conservation of momentum:

total momentum before = total momentum after

$\Rightarrow \quad 5 \times 2 + 6 \times (-4) = 2v + 6 \times (-2)$

$\Rightarrow \quad -14 = 2v - 12$

$\Rightarrow \quad 2v = -2$

$v = -1\,\text{m}\,\text{s}^{-1}$

So the final velocity of A is $1\,\text{m}\,\text{s}^{-1}$ in the opposite direction to its original motion.

Total initial K.E. $= \frac{1}{2} \times 2 \times 5^2 + \frac{1}{2} \times 6 \times 4^2 = 73\,\text{J}$

Remember kinetic energy is a scalar – so it doesn't matter that the spheres are moving in opposite directions.

Total final K.E. $= \frac{1}{2} \times 2 \times 1^2 + \frac{1}{2} \times 6 \times 2^2 = 13\,\text{J}$

Loss in K.E. $= 73\,\text{J} - 13\,\text{J} = -60\,\text{J}$

A common mistake is to try to use kinetic energy before = kinetic energy after to solve problems on collisions. This is wrong because energy is usually lost as heat and sound.

Sometimes the objects involved in a collision are not moving along the same straight line, in which case you will need to express the velocities using **i** and **j** components or column vectors.

EXAMPLE 2

Two ice-skaters, Andrew (of mass 80 kg) and Bella (of mass 40 kg), slide towards each other on smooth horizontal ice. Andrew has a speed of $2\,\text{m}\,\text{s}^{-1}$ in the **i** direction and Bella has a speed of $4\,\text{m}\,\text{s}^{-1}$ in the direction shown in the diagram.

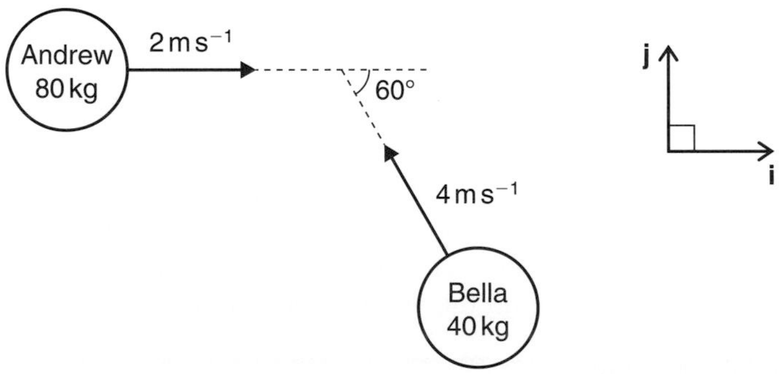

i) Calculate the initial momentum of each ice-skater.

The ice-skaters collide and embrace. After the collision the skaters move off together with a common velocity of $(u\mathbf{i} + v\mathbf{j})\,\text{m}\,\text{s}^{-1}$.

ii) Find u and v.

iii) Find the angle between the final direction of motion and the **i** direction.

SOLUTION

i) Andrew: momentum $= m\mathbf{v}$

$$= 80 \times \begin{pmatrix} 2 \\ 0 \end{pmatrix}$$

Use vector notation as Andrew and Bella aren't travelling along the same straight line.

$$= \begin{pmatrix} 160 \\ 0 \end{pmatrix} \text{ Ns or } 160\mathbf{i} \text{ Ns}$$

Bella: momentum $= m\mathbf{v}$

$$= 40 \times \begin{pmatrix} -4\cos 60^\circ \\ 4\sin 60^\circ \end{pmatrix}$$

Take care with your signs – Bella is travelling in the negative **i** direction!

$$= \begin{pmatrix} -80 \\ 80\sqrt{3} \end{pmatrix} \text{ Ns or } (-80\mathbf{i} + 80\sqrt{3}\mathbf{j}) \text{ Ns}$$

ii) Using the law of conservation of momentum:

total momentum before = total momentum after

$$\begin{pmatrix} 160 \\ 0 \end{pmatrix} + \begin{pmatrix} -80 \\ 80\sqrt{3} \end{pmatrix} = 120\begin{pmatrix} u \\ v \end{pmatrix}$$

$$\begin{pmatrix} 80 \\ 80\sqrt{3} \end{pmatrix} = \begin{pmatrix} 120u \\ 120v \end{pmatrix}$$

$$\Rightarrow \quad 80 = 120u$$

Equate the top line of each vector (**i** components)...

$$u = \frac{2}{3}$$

$$\Rightarrow \quad 80\sqrt{3} = 120v$$

...then equate the bottom line of each vector (**j** components).

$$v = \frac{2\sqrt{3}}{3}$$

iii) To find the direction of motion you should draw a triangle.

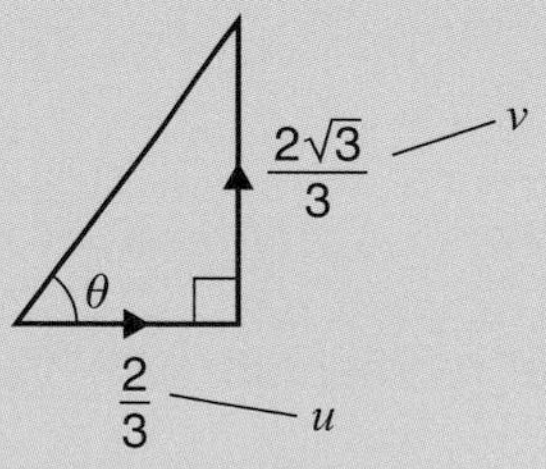

$$\tan\theta = \frac{\frac{2\sqrt{3}}{3}}{\frac{2}{3}} = \frac{2\sqrt{3}}{3} \times \frac{3}{2} = \sqrt{3}$$

$$\Rightarrow \theta = 60^\circ$$

Momentum is also conserved when parts of an object separate, as in the next example.

EXAMPLE 3

Amir (mass 60 kg) and Sam (mass 45 kg) are both standing on a skateboard of mass 5 kg. The skateboard is initially at rest on a horizontal surface when Amir jumps off the skateboard with a speed of $3\,\mathrm{m\,s^{-1}}$. Find the velocity of Sam and the skateboard immediately after Amir's jump.

SOLUTION

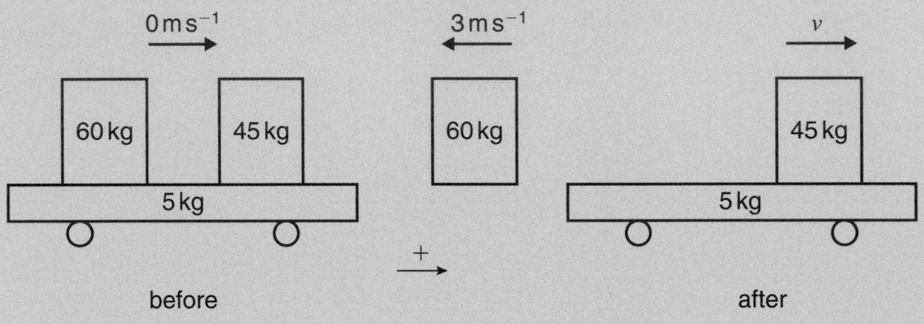

Initially the skateboard is at rest so the momentum is 0 Ns.

Using the law of conservation of momentum:

$$\text{momentum before} = \text{momentum after}$$

$$0 = 60 \times (-3) + 50v$$

$$\Rightarrow \quad 50v = 180$$

$$\Rightarrow \quad v = 3.6\,\mathrm{m\,s^{-1}}$$

LINKS

Mechanics — Angular momentum (M4), Variable mass (M4).

Test Yourself

1 Two miniature trains, P of mass 3 kg and speed 8 m s^{-1}, and Q of mass 2 kg and speed 6 m s^{-1}, move in the same direction along a smooth horizontal track. The trains collide and couple together. Find the final speed of the two trains.

A 7.2 m s^{-1} **B** 2.4 m s^{-1} **C** 10.56 m s^{-1} **D** 12 m s^{-1}

2 Two identical ice pucks, S and T, each of mass m kg, slide towards each other on smooth horizontal ice, as shown in the diagram below. The two pucks collide and coalesce. After the collision, the combined object moves with a velocity of $(u\mathbf{i} + v\mathbf{j})$ m s^{-1}. Find u and v.

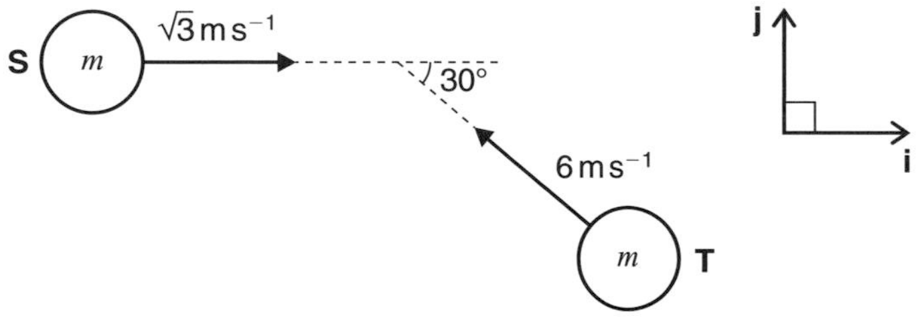

A $u = 4\sqrt{3}$ and $v = 1.5$ **B** $u = -\sqrt{3}$ and $v = 1.5$

C $u = -2\sqrt{3}$ and $v = 3$ **D** $u = -1.27$ and $v = 3\sqrt{3}$

3 A firework of mass 0.6 kg has a velocity of $(4\mathbf{i} + 10\mathbf{j})$ m s^{-1} when it explodes into two parts, F and G. Part F has a mass of 0.1 kg and a velocity of $(-2\mathbf{i} + 6\mathbf{j})$ m s^{-1}. Find the velocity of part G.

A $(2.2\mathbf{i} + 6.6\mathbf{j})$ m s^{-1} **B** $(1.3\mathbf{i} + 2.7\mathbf{j})$ m s^{-1}

C $(2.6\mathbf{i} + 5.4\mathbf{j})$ m s^{-1} **D** $(5.2\mathbf{i} + 10.8\mathbf{j})$ m s^{-1}

Exam-Style Question

Two small discs, A of mass m kg and speed $4u$ m s^{-1}, and B of mass $2m$ kg and speed u m s^{-1}, are moving towards each other on the same straight line along a smooth horizontal plane. The two discs collide head on and disc A subsequently moves with speed $\frac{u}{2}$ m s^{-1} in the same direction to its original motion, while disc B moves with speed V m s^{-1}.

i) Show that $V = \frac{3u}{4}$.

ii) Hence express the final kinetic energy as a fraction of the original kinetic energy.

For the rest of this question, take the value of u to be 1, so $v = \frac{3}{4}$.

iii) A third disc, C, of mass m kg is moving with velocity $\begin{pmatrix} 3 \\ 6 \end{pmatrix}$ m s^{-1}. After the collision between A and B, C collides with B. B and C coalesce and move off together with velocity $\mathbf{V}$ m s^{-1}. Find the magnitude and direction of $\mathbf{V}$.

Impact

A ABOUT THIS TOPIC

If you were to drop a perfectly bouncy ball, it would rebound to the height from which you dropped it; so its rebound speed would equal the speed with which it hit the ground. However, if you dropped a stone on to some sand, it wouldn't rebound at all. Most impacts lie somewhere in between these two extremes and this section deals with the relationship between the impact speed and the rebound speed of objects in collisions.

R REMEMBER

- Mechanical energy from M2.
- Law of conservation of momentum from M2.

K KEY FACTS

- In questions involving impact, two laws apply: the law of conservation of momentum and Newton's experimental law.
- Newton's experimental law states

  speed of separation $= e \times$ speed of approach

  where e is the coefficient of restitution.
- e is a constant and lies between 0 and 1.
- When no kinetic energy is lost, a collision is said to be **perfectly elastic** and $e = 1$, so in this special case

  speed of separation $=$ speed of approach
- When all the mechanical energy is lost in a collision it is said to be **perfectly inelastic** and $e = 0$, so the speed of separation is zero.

Collisions

You will meet two types of problem. One is where a single object collides with a fixed surface and the other is where two objects collide.

This section will only deal with situations where the object hits the surface at right angles.

For impact with a fixed surface:

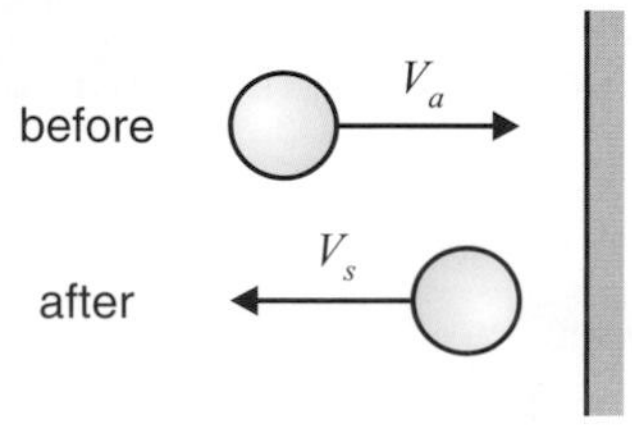

speed of separation $= e \times$ speed of approach

$\Rightarrow \qquad V_s = e \times V_a$

EXAMPLE 1

A tennis ball is dropped from a height of 2 m and rebounds to a height of 1.5 m. Find the coefficient of restitution between the ball and the ground.

SOLUTION

You need to find the speed with which the ball hits the ground and its rebound speed.

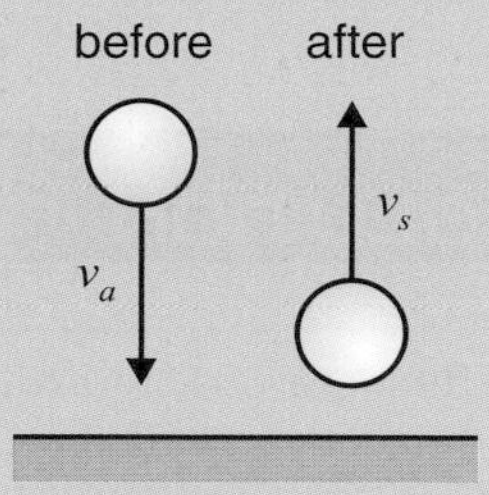

Before impact: 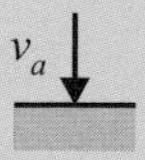 $u = 0\,\text{m s}^{-1}, a = g\,\text{m s}^{-2}, s = 2\,\text{m}$ and $v = v_a$

The ball is dropped.

Using $v^2 = u^2 + 2as$ gives: $v_a^{\,2} = 0 + 2 \times g \times 2 = 39.2$

Store the exact values in your calculator.

$\Rightarrow \quad v_a = 6.2609\ldots\,\text{m s}^{-1}$

At max height, the speed is $0\,\text{m s}^{-1}$.

After impact: 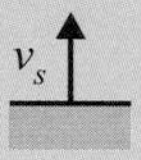 $v = 0\,\text{m s}^{-1}, a = -g\,\text{m s}^{-2}, s = 1.5\,\text{m}$ and $u = v_s$

Using $v^2 = u^2 + 2as$ gives: $0 = v_s^{\,2} - 2 \times g \times 1.5$

$\Rightarrow \quad v_s^{\,2} = 29.4$

$\Rightarrow \quad v_s = 5.4221\ldots\,\text{m s}^{-1}$

Restitution: using Newton's experimental law

speed of separation = $e \times$ speed of approach

$$\Rightarrow \quad e = \frac{v_s}{v_a}$$

e doesn't have any units, as it is the ratio of two speeds.

$$\Rightarrow \quad e = \frac{5.4221\ldots}{6.2609\ldots} = 0.866 \text{ (to 3 s.f.)}$$

Make sure that you have the formula the right way around – the speed of separation will always be less than (or equal to) the speed of approach.

For impact between two objects:

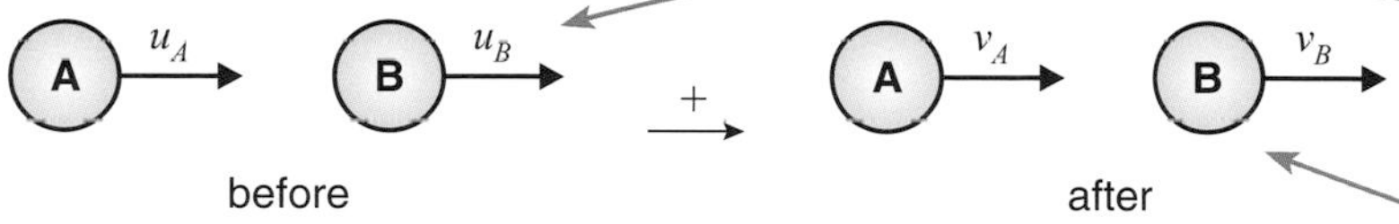

The two objects are approaching each other with speed $u_A - u_B$.

The two objects are separating with speed $v_B - v_A$.

speed of separation = $e \times$ speed of approach

$\Rightarrow \quad v_B - v_A = e \times (u_A - u_B)$

A ADVICE

Note that before the impact, object A must catch up with B otherwise they wouldn't collide, so $u_A > u_B$. After the impact, object B must move away from A, so $v_B > v_A$.

EXAMPLE 2

A marble of mass m kg is travelling with a speed of $5\,m\,s^{-1}$, when it collides directly with a stationary marble of mass $2m$ kg. The coefficient of restitution between the two marbles is 0.8. Find the speeds and directions of the two marbles after the collision.

SOLUTION

The word 'directly' in the question means that marble A is moving along the straight line between the centres of the two marbles.

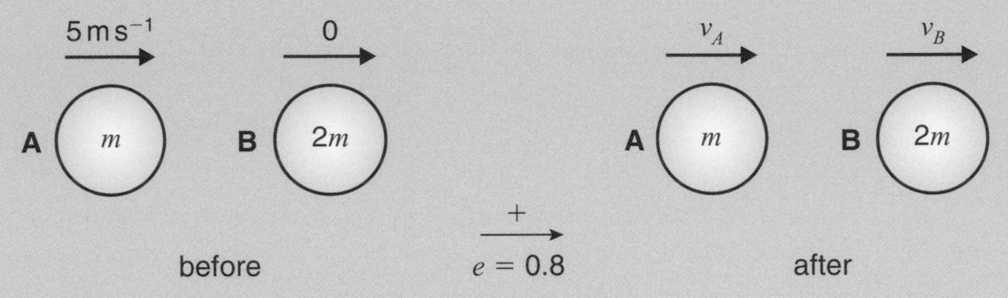

There are two unknowns to find (v_A and v_B) and so you need to form two equations.

Conservation of momentum (→): ← This gives the first equation.

$$\text{momentum before} = \text{momentum after}$$

$$\Rightarrow \quad m \times 5 + 2m \times 0 = m \times v_A + 2m \times v_B$$

$$\Rightarrow \quad 5m = mv_A + 2mv_B$$

Dividing through by m: $\quad 5 = v_A + 2v_B \quad$ ①

Restitution: ← This gives the second equation.

$$\text{speed of separation} = e \times \text{speed of approach}$$

$$\Rightarrow \quad v_B - v_A = 0.8 \times 5$$

The speed of approach is $u_A - u_B$ or $5 - 0 = 5$.

$$\Rightarrow \quad v_B - v_A = 4 \quad ②$$

Solve equations ① and ② simultaneously:

$$\begin{aligned} 5 &= v_A + 2v_B \quad ①\\ +\ 4 &= -v_A + v_B \quad ②\\ \hline 9 &= 3v_B \end{aligned}$$

So $v_B = 3$

Substituting $v_B = 3$ into either equation ① or ② gives $v_A = -1\,m\,s^{-1}$.

So marble B has a speed of $3\,m\,s^{-1}$ in marble A's original direction of motion and marble A has a speed of $1\,m\,s^{-1}$ in the opposite direction.

A ADVICE

When two objects collide you need to be extra careful with your signs as it is easy to make mistakes. The easiest way to avoid sign errors is to take all the velocities in the same direction, so if an object is travelling in the opposite direction its velocity is negative.

EXAMPLE 3

Two spheres, P of mass 6 kg and Q of mass 3 kg, are moving in the same straight line along a horizontal plane with velocities as shown in the diagram. The spheres collide head on, and after the collision P continues in the same direction with a speed of $1\,\text{m s}^{-1}$.

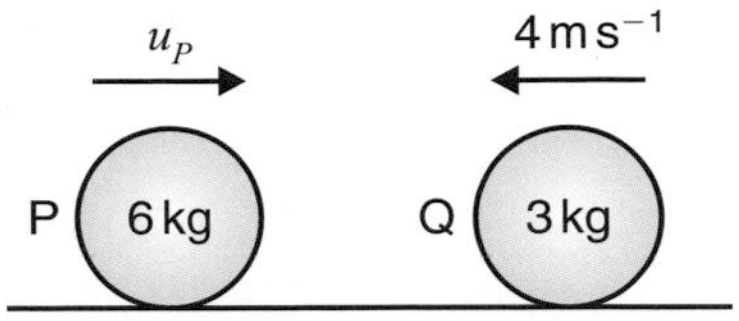

i) Find the initial velocity of P and the final velocity of Q given the coefficient of restitution between the two spheres is $\frac{1}{2}$.

ii) Calculate the energy lost in the collision.

SOLUTION

Draw a 'before' and 'after' diagram. Show clearly the positive direction.

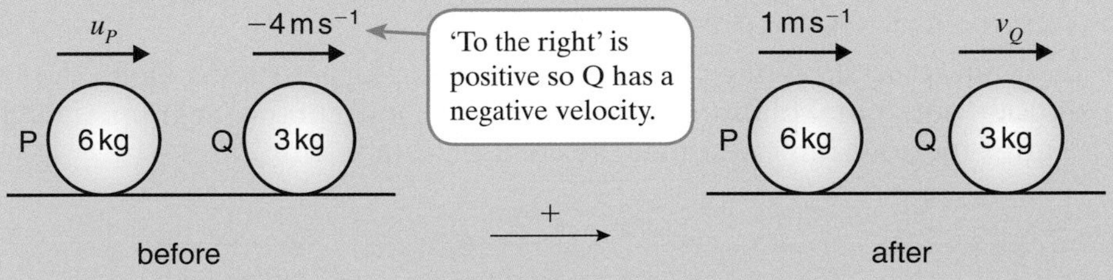

i) There are two unknowns to find (u_P and v_Q) and so you need to form two equations.

Conservation of momentum (→): ← This gives the first equation.

momentum before = momentum after

$\Rightarrow \quad 6 \times u_P + 3 \times (-4) = 6 \times 1 + 3 \times v_Q$

$\Rightarrow \quad 6u_P - 12 = 6 + 3v_Q$

Rearranging: $\quad 6u_P - 3v_Q = 18 \quad$ ①

Restitution: ← Newton's experimental law gives the second equation.

Treat the spheres as though they are moving in the same direction, so the speed of approach is $u_P - u_Q$. →

speed of separation = e × speed of approach

$\Rightarrow \quad v_Q - 1 = \frac{1}{2} \times (u_P - (-4))$

Multiplying through by 2: $2v_Q - 2 = u_P + 4$

Rearranging: $\quad 2v_Q - u_P = 6 \quad$ ②

Solve equations ① and ② simultaneously:

$$\begin{aligned} 6u_P - 3v_Q &= 18 \quad ① \\ + \; -6u_P + 12v_Q &= 36 \quad ② \times 6 \\ \hline 9v_Q &= 54 \end{aligned}$$

So $v_Q = 6\,\text{m s}^{-1}$

Substituting $v_Q = 6$ into equation ① or ② gives $u_P = 6\,\text{m s}^{-1}$.

So before the collision, sphere P has a speed of $6\,\text{m s}^{-1}$ in the opposite direction to sphere Q's initial direction.

After the collision, the direction of Q is reversed and it moves with a speed of $6\,\text{m s}^{-1}$.

ii) K.E. before $= \frac{1}{2} \times 6 \times 6^2 + \frac{1}{2} \times 3 \times 4^2 = 132\,\text{J}$

K.E. after $= \frac{1}{2} \times 6 \times 1^2 + \frac{1}{2} \times 3 \times 6^2 = 57\,\text{J}$

Loss in K.E. $= 132 - 57 = 75\,\text{J}$

The 'lost' energy will have been converted into heat and sound.

LINKS

Mechanics — Angular momentum (M4), Variable mass (M4).

Test Yourself

1 A van, of mass 2000 kg, is travelling at 20 m s^{-1} when it collides directly with a car of mass 1200 kg travelling at 15 m s^{-1} in the same direction. After the collision the car has a speed of 18.25 m s^{-1}. Find the speed of the van after the collision and hence the coefficient of restitution between the two vehicles.

A 1 **B** 1.825 **C** 0.32 **D** 0.533

2 A bouncy ball is dropped from a height of 4 m. Find the mechanical energy immediately after the impact as a fraction of the ball's original energy, given that the coefficient of restitution between the ball and the ground is $\frac{3}{4}$.

A $\frac{9}{16}$ **B** $\frac{7}{16}$ **C** 9 **D** $\frac{3}{4}$

3 Two small discs, P of mass 3 kg and Q of mass 2 kg are sliding along the same straight line on a smooth, horizontal plane with the velocities shown in the diagram. Calculate the velocities of P and Q after the collision given that the coefficient of restitution is $\frac{3}{4}$.

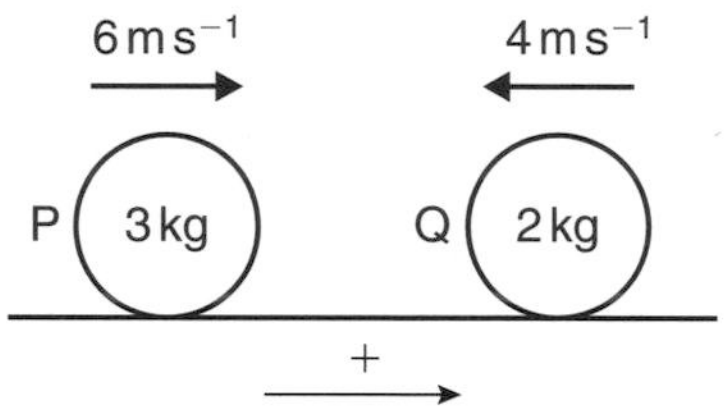

A $v_P = 4.6$ m s^{-1} and $v_Q = 6.1$ m s^{-1} **B** $v_P = 2.2$ m s^{-1} and $v_Q = 9.7$ m s^{-1}

C $v_P = 1.4$ m s^{-1} and $v_Q = 2.9$ m s^{-1} **D** $v_P = -1$ m s^{-1} and $v_Q = 6.5$ m s^{-1}

Exam-Style Question

i) A white snooker ball is moving with a speed of u m s^{-1} when it collides with a stationary red ball. The two balls have the same mass, m kg. The coefficient of restitution between the two balls is $\frac{4}{5}$, and the two balls travel along the same straight line after the collision. Show that after the collision the red ball has speed $\frac{9u}{10}$ m s^{-1} and find the velocity of the white ball in terms of u.

ii) After the collision in part **i)**, the red ball moves on to have a perfectly elastic collision with a side cushion and rebounds. The red ball then collides again with the white ball. The motion is all along the same straight line.

A) Find the impulse which acts on the cushion.

B) Show that the red ball is stationary after its second collision with the white ball and find the velocity of the white ball in terms of u.

Oblique impact

A ABOUT THIS TOPIC

In the last section you solved problems involving objects colliding with a surface which is perpendicular to the object's direction of motion. However, in real-life situations, an object often collides with a surface obliquely – an oblique angle is any angle which is not 90° (or a multiple of 90°) – for example, when a golf ball hits the ground.

R REMEMBER

- Resolving velocities from M1.
- Kinetic energy from M2.
- Impulse from M2.
- Newton's law of impact from M2.

K KEY FACTS

- An oblique impact is one where an object collides with a plane at an angle which is not 90°.
- In any impact – including oblique impacts – the impulse acts at right angles to the plane.
- In an oblique impact there is no impulse, no change in momentum and no change in velocity parallel to the plane.

Impulse in oblique impacts

When an object collides with a smooth plane, the impulse is perpendicular to the plane.

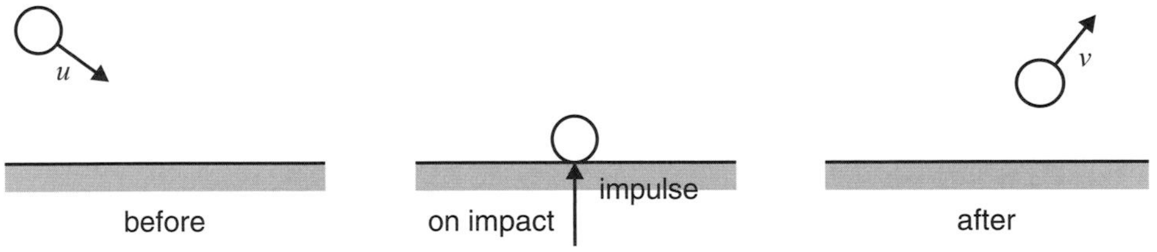

There is **no** impulse parallel to the plane. As impulse = change in momentum, there is no momentum change (or for that matter, velocity change) parallel to the plane. So, when you resolve the velocity of the object into components (parallel and perpendicular to the plane), the component of the velocity **parallel** to the plane is the **same** before and after impact.

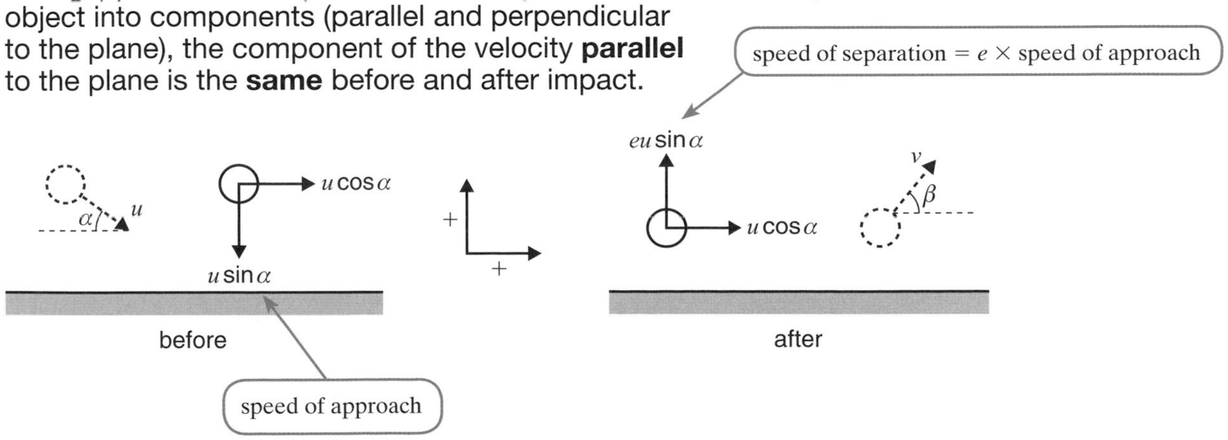

The next examples show you how to solve problems involving oblique impacts.

EXAMPLE 1

A disc of mass 0.1 kg slides on a smooth horizontal surface at a speed of $15\,\mathrm{m\,s^{-1}}$ when it collides with a smooth barrier inclined at an angle of 30° to the disc's direction of motion. The coefficient of restitution is 0.8. Find the following.

i) The final speed and direction of motion of the disc.

ii) The impulse which acts on the disc.

SOLUTION

i) First draw 'before' and 'after' diagrams.

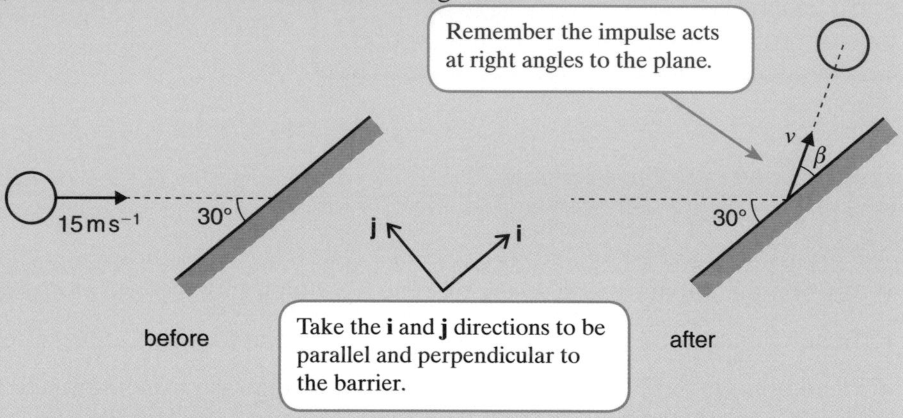

Resolve the velocity into components parallel and perpendicular to the plane:

Before impact:

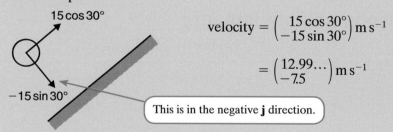

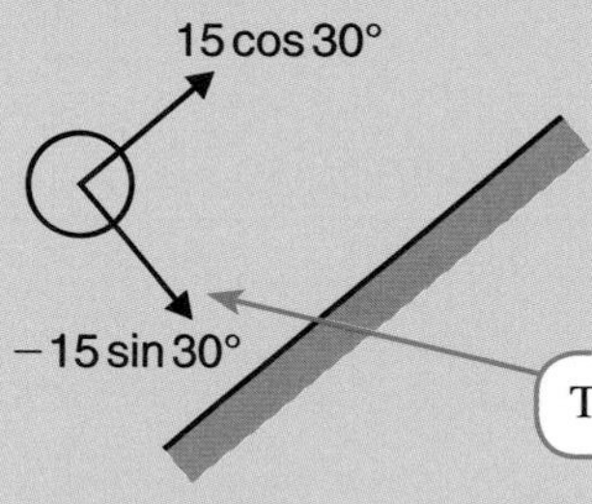

$$\text{velocity} = \begin{pmatrix} 15\cos 30° \\ -15\sin 30° \end{pmatrix}\mathrm{m\,s^{-1}}$$

$$= \begin{pmatrix} 12.99\ldots \\ -7.5 \end{pmatrix}\mathrm{m\,s^{-1}}$$

This is in the negative **j** direction.

Restitution:
After impact:

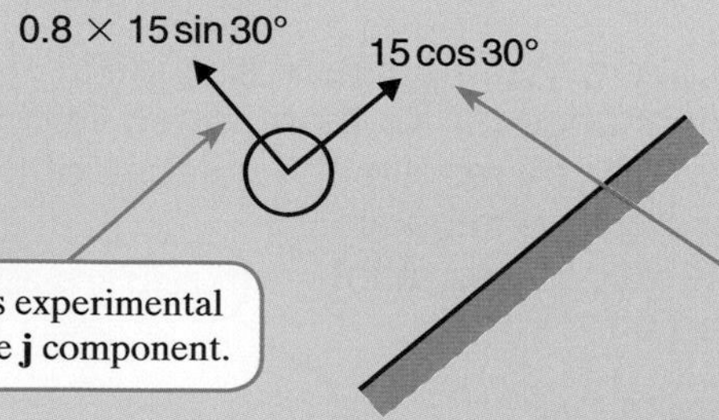

$$\text{velocity} = \begin{pmatrix} 15\cos 30° \\ 0.8 \times 15\sin 30° \end{pmatrix}\mathrm{m\,s^{-1}}$$

$$= \begin{pmatrix} 12.99\ldots \\ 6 \end{pmatrix}\mathrm{m\,s^{-1}}$$

Use Newton's experimental law to find the **j** component.

The component of the velocity parallel to the plane is unchanged.

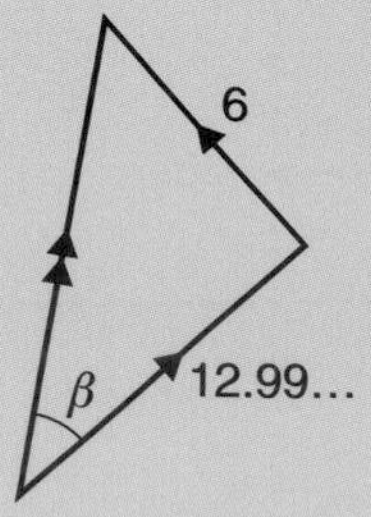

Draw a triangle to help you find the speed and direction of the disc after the impact.

speed $= \sqrt{12.99\ldots^2 + 6^2} = 14.3\,\mathrm{m\,s^{-1}}$ to 3 s.f.

direction: $\tan\beta = \dfrac{6}{12.99\ldots} \Rightarrow \beta = 24.8°$ to 3 s.f.

ii) impulse = final momentum − initial momentum

$$= 0.1 \times \begin{pmatrix} 12.99\ldots \\ 6 \end{pmatrix} - 0.1 \times \begin{pmatrix} 12.99\ldots \\ -7.5 \end{pmatrix}$$

$$= \begin{pmatrix} 0 \\ 1.35 \end{pmatrix} \text{Ns}$$

So the impulse on the disc is 1.35 Ns perpendicular to the plane in the **j** direction.

EXAMPLE 2

A small ball is projected horizontally over the edge of a table 1 m high with a speed of 5 m s^{-1}. The ball bounces on smooth horizontal ground. The speed of the ball immediately after its first impact with the ground is 5.66 m s^{-1}.

Calculate the coefficient of restitution between the ball and the ground and find the angle with the ground at which the ball travels immediately after the bounce.

SOLUTION

First draw a diagram.

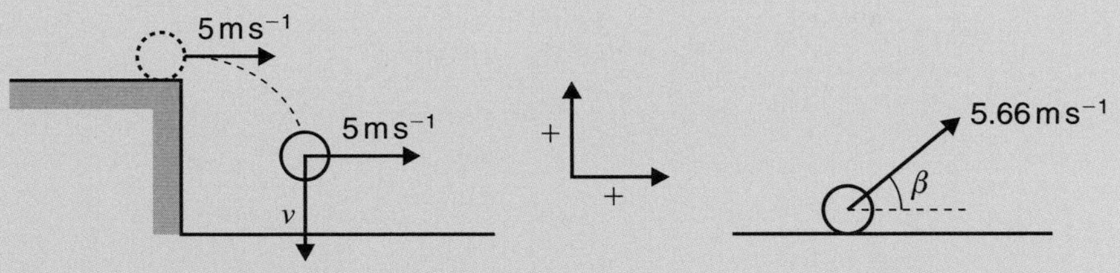

before after

Remember that the impulse only acts at right angles to the ground, and so you only need to work out the vertical component of the velocity before and after impact.

To find the coefficient of restitution you need to know the vertical component of the velocity before and after impact. You can find the vertical component of the velocity immediately before the impact using $v^2 = u^2 + 2as$:

Initially there is no vertical component to the ball's velocity.

Substituting $u = 0, a = 9.8, s = 1$ gives $v^2 = 0 + 2 \times 9.8 \times 1$

$$\Rightarrow v = 4.27\ldots$$

After the impact the velocity is $\begin{pmatrix} 5 \\ e \times 4.27\ldots \end{pmatrix}$ m s^{-1}:

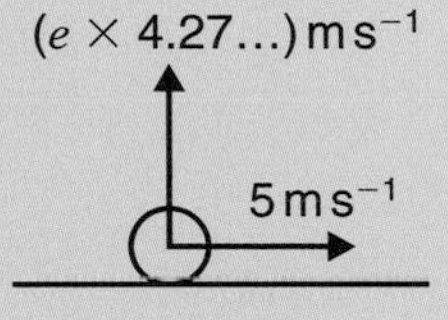

after

The speed is given as 5.66 m s^{-1}.

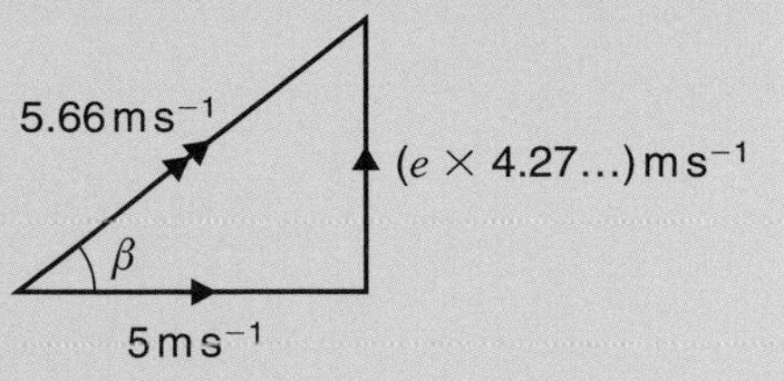

Using Pythagoras' theorem

$5^2 + (e \times 4.27\ldots)^2 = 5.66^2$

$\Rightarrow \quad e^2 = \dfrac{5.66^2 - 5^2}{4.27\ldots^2}$

$\Rightarrow \quad e = 0.6$ to 1 d.p.

For the angle: $\cos\beta = \dfrac{5}{5.66}$

$\beta = 27.9°$ (to 1 d.p.)

Use cos because that involves the two 'sides' that you were given in the question.

EXAMPLE 3

A ball of mass m moving with velocity $\begin{pmatrix} u \\ -v \end{pmatrix}$ m s^{-1} bounces off a smooth plane as shown in the diagram.

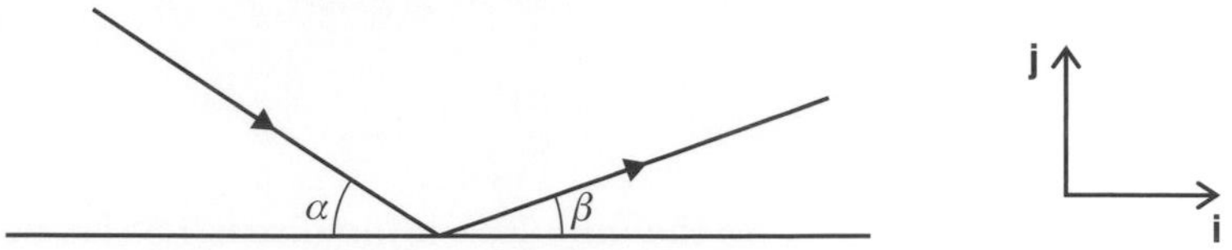

The coefficient of restitution between the ball and the plane is e.

i) Find the impulse acting on the ball.

ii) Show that $\tan \beta = e \tan \alpha$.

iii) Find the loss in kinetic energy.

SOLUTION

i) To find the impulse you need to work out the final velocity of the ball.

Restitution (↑):

The impulse only acts in the **j**-direction.

speed of separation = $e \times$ speed of approach

$= ev$

So the velocity of the ball after the impact is $\begin{pmatrix} u \\ ev \end{pmatrix}$ m s^{-1}.

There is no impulse parallel to the plane (the **i** direction), so the velocity parallel to the plane is unchanged.

Now use the equation

impulse = final momentum − initial momentum

$$= m\begin{pmatrix} u \\ ev \end{pmatrix} - m\begin{pmatrix} u \\ -v \end{pmatrix}$$

$$= \begin{pmatrix} mu \\ mev \end{pmatrix} - \begin{pmatrix} mu \\ -mv \end{pmatrix}$$

$$= \begin{pmatrix} 0 \\ mev + mv \end{pmatrix}$$

$$= \begin{pmatrix} 0 \\ mv(e+1) \end{pmatrix} \text{ Ns}$$

ii) After the impact the ball moves with velocity $\begin{pmatrix} u \\ ev \end{pmatrix}$ m s^{-1}.

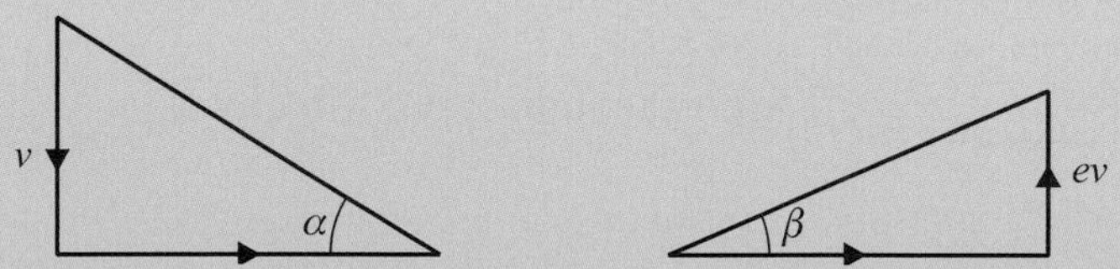

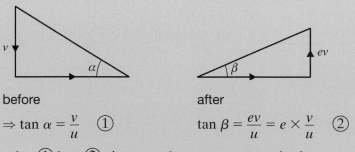

before

$\Rightarrow \tan \alpha = \dfrac{v}{u}$ ①

after

$\tan \beta = \dfrac{ev}{u} = e \times \dfrac{v}{u}$ ②

Substituting ① into ② gives: $\tan \beta = e \tan \alpha$ as required.

iii) Velocity before $= \begin{pmatrix} u \\ -v \end{pmatrix}$ m s^{-1} $\Rightarrow$ K.E. before $= \frac{1}{2}m(u^2 + v^2)$

Velocity after $= \begin{pmatrix} u \\ ev \end{pmatrix}$ m s^{-1} $\Rightarrow$ K.E. after $= \frac{1}{2}m(u^2 + (ev)^2)$

So loss in K.E. $= \frac{1}{2}m(u^2 + v^2) - \frac{1}{2}m(u^2 + (ev)^2)$

$= \frac{1}{2}mv^2 - \frac{1}{2}me^2v^2$

$= \frac{1}{2}mv^2(1 - e^2)$

Notice when $e = 1$ then $(1 - e^2) = 0$. So for a **perfectly elastic** collision, no K.E. is lost so the final K.E. is equal to the inital K.E.

Also, when $e = 0$ the $(1 - e^2) = 1$. So for a **perfectly inelastic** collision the loss in K.E. is $\frac{1}{2}mv^2$.

R RULE

The above example gives you the useful result that when an object collides with a plane at an angle α and rebounds at an angle β then:

$$\tan \beta = e \tan \alpha$$

You can see that when $e = 1$ then $\tan \beta = \tan \alpha$. So for elastic collisions $\alpha = \beta$.

LINKS

Mechanics — Angular momentum (M4), Variable mass (M4).

Test Yourself

1 A ball moving with velocity $\begin{pmatrix}4\\5\end{pmatrix}$ m s^{-1} collides with a smooth barrier which lies in the direction $\begin{pmatrix}0\\1\end{pmatrix}$.

The coefficient of restitution between the ball and the barrier is 0.5.

Find the velocity of the ball immediately after the impact.

A $\begin{pmatrix}-2\\-2.5\end{pmatrix}$ m s^{-1} **B** $\begin{pmatrix}2\\5\end{pmatrix}$ m s^{-1} **C** $\begin{pmatrix}4\\-2.5\end{pmatrix}$ m s^{-1} **D** $\begin{pmatrix}-2\\5\end{pmatrix}$ m s^{-1}

2 A disc collides with a smooth barrier at 60° to its direction of motion. The speed of the disc immediately before the collision is 12 m s^{-1} and after the collision is 8 m s^{-1}. Calculate the coefficient of restitution for the impact.

A $e - \frac{2}{3}$ **B** $e = 0.509$ **C** $e = 0.259$ **D** $e = 0.577$

3 A skater is sliding on smooth horizontal ice. While moving at 2 m s^{-1}, the skater drops a small ball from a height of 0.5 m above the ice. The coefficient of restitution for the impact between the ball and the ice is 0.4. At what angle to the horizontal does the ball rebound from the ice?

A 32.1° **B** 57.4° **C** 21.8° **D** 75.7°

Exam-Style Question

A small ball, of mass 0.1 kg, bounces off a smooth horizontal plane. The ball hits the plane with a speed of $15\,\mathrm{m\,s^{-1}}$ at an angle of $\arcsin\frac{4}{5}$ to the plane.

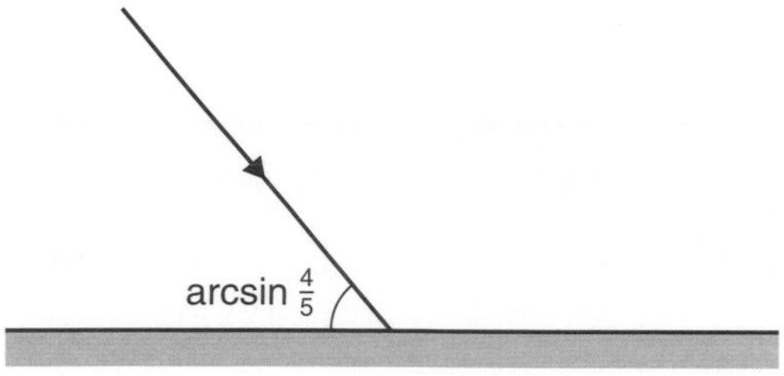

i) Find the speed with which the ball rebounds from the plane and the loss of kinetic energy in each of the following cases.

A) The collision is perfectly elastic

B) The collision is perfectly inelastic

ii) In another case, the ball rebounds at an angle of $\arcsin\frac{3}{5}$ to the plane.

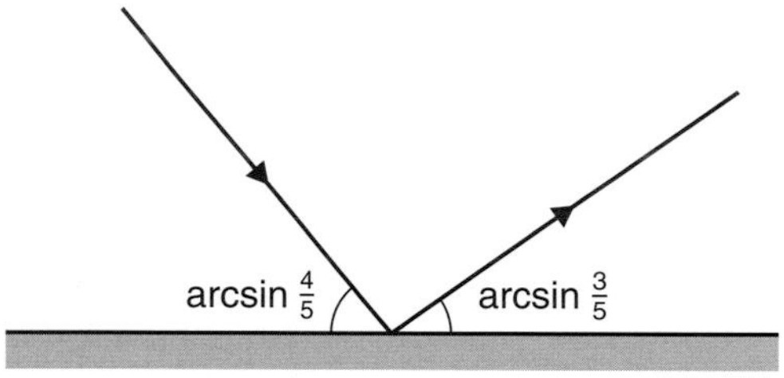

Find the speed with which the ball rebounds from the plane, loss of kinetic energy and coefficient of restitution in this case.

Frameworks

7

▶▶ 157

Light frameworks

A ABOUT THIS TOPIC

In the second section of this book you met the idea of the equilibrium of a rigid body and the conditions needed to test for equilibrium. This section introduces you to a particular example of equilibrium. It is concerned with structures that are known as *frameworks*. A framework consists of light rigid rods, which are jointed together smoothly; this is described as *pin-jointed*.

R REMEMBER

- Forces and resolution of forces from M1.
- Conditions for equilibrium under a set of concurrent forces from M1.
- Moment of a force from M2.
- Conditions for the equilibrium of a rigid body from M2.

K KEY FACTS

- A framework is a structure made of light rigid rods, jointed together smoothly at the ends.
- Assumptions
  - All members of the framework are light rods, so their masses can be ignored.
  - All the joints are smooth, so there are no moments acting on them.
- Consequence of these assumptions
  - All the internal forces are directed along the rods – there are two possibilities to consider:

    1 The rod is in **tension** when the forces pull inwards from both ends.

    2 The rod is in **compression (thrust)** when the forces push out from the centre of the rod.

  - In both cases the forces acting on each end of the rod are equal and opposite.
- **Method for solving framework problems**
  - First calculate the **external** forces acting on a framework.

    1 Consider the horizontal and vertical equilibrium of the whole framework.

    2 Take moments about a suitable point for the whole framework.
  - Then consider the equilibrium of each joint in turn in order to find the **internal** forces.

EXAMPLE 1

The diagram shows a framework made up of three light rods which are freely jointed at A, B and C. Their lengths (in metres) are shown on the diagram. The framework rests on two smooth supports at B and C and supports a load of 5000 N at A.

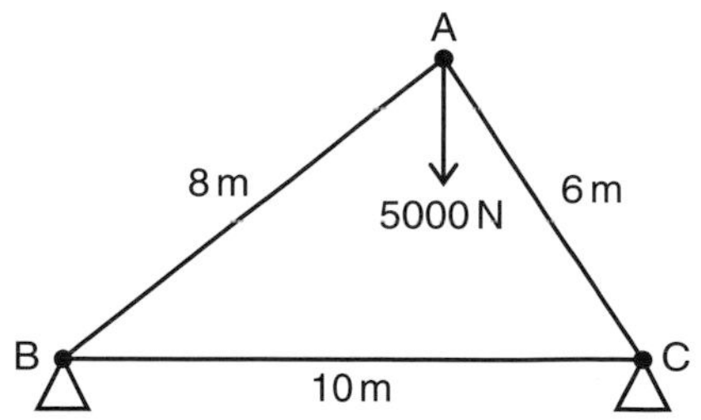

i) Find the reactions at B and C.

ii) Find the forces in each of the rods AB, AC and BC, stating whether the rod is in tension or compression.

SOLUTION

i) The first stage in solving any problem with frameworks is to draw a diagram that includes all the external and internal forces. At this stage you are unlikely to know whether the internal forces are tensions or compressions. This does not matter. If you are consistent and put in all the internal forces as tensions, a negative answer will indicate that the rod is in compression and not tension.

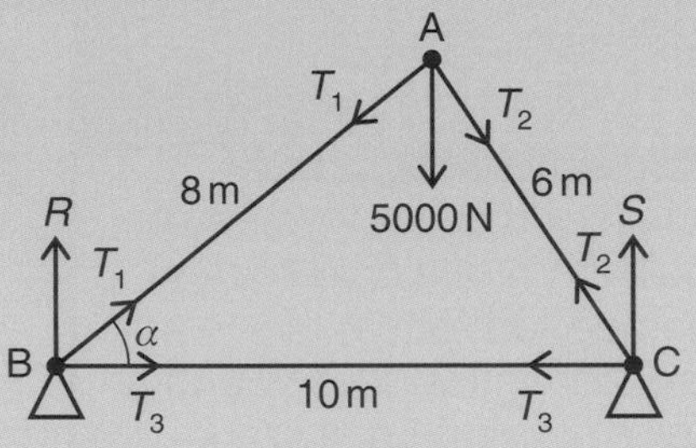

External forces

There are three external forces acting on the framework, R N and S N vertically upwards and 5000 N downwards. Looking at the equilibrium of the structure as a whole:

For vertical equilibrium (↑): $\quad R + S - 5000 = 0 \quad$ ①

Taking moments about B (↺): $\quad 10 \times S - (8\cos\alpha) \times 5000 = 0$

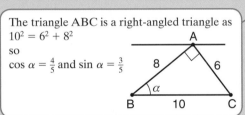

The triangle ABC is a right-angled triangle as $10^2 = 6^2 + 8^2$

so

$\cos\alpha = \frac{4}{5}$ and $\sin\alpha = \frac{3}{5}$

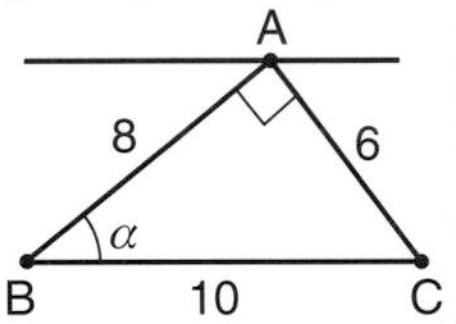

$\Rightarrow \quad S = 3200\,\text{N}$

From ① $\quad R = 1800\,\text{N}$

So the answer to part **i)** is that the reactions at B and C are 1800 N and 3200 N respectively.

ii) Internal forces

The next step is to consider the equilibrium at each joint in turn.

Starting with B:

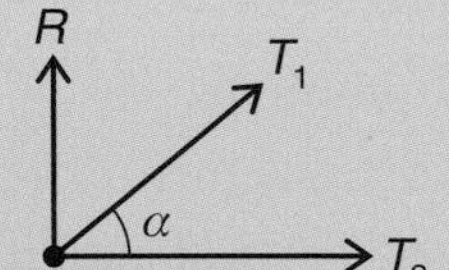

Vertical equilibrium (↑): $R + T_1 \sin\alpha = 0$

$\Rightarrow \quad 1800 + \frac{3}{5}T_1 = 0$

$\Rightarrow \quad T_1 = -3000\,\text{N}$ (compression)

Horizontal equilibrium (→): $T_1 \cos\alpha + T_3 = 0$

$\Rightarrow \quad T_3 = 3000 \times \frac{4}{5} = 2400\,\text{N}$ (tension)

Now look at C:

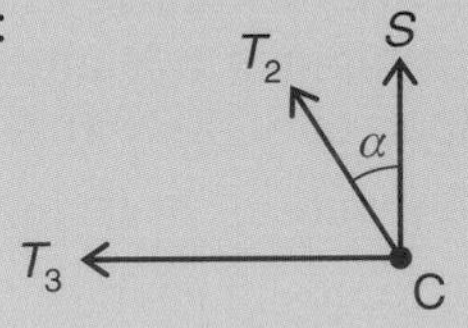

Horizontal equilibrium: $T_2 \sin\alpha + T_3 = 0$

$\Rightarrow \quad \frac{3}{5}T_2 + 2400 = 0$

$\Rightarrow \quad T_2 = -4000\,\text{N}$ (compression)

So the answer to part **ii)** is that rod BC has a tension of 2400 N, rod AB has a compression of 3000 N and rod AC has a compression of 4000 N.

Check

Check whether these answers work at joint A.

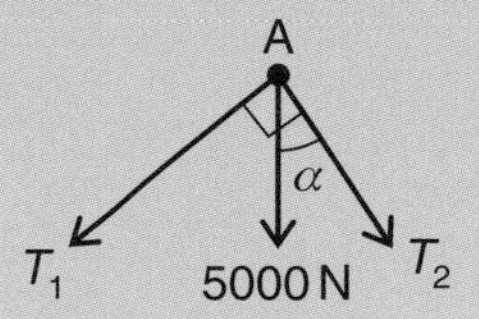

Horizontal equilibrium(→):

$-T_1\cos\alpha + T_2\sin\alpha = -(-3000)\times\frac{4}{5} + (-4000)\times\frac{3}{5} = 0$ ✓

Vertical equilibrium (↑):

$-T_1\sin\alpha - T_2\cos\alpha - 5000 = -(-3000)\times\frac{3}{5} - (-4000)\times\frac{4}{5} - 5000 = 0$ ✓

So the joint at A is in equilibrium (as you would hope).

EXAMPLE 2

The diagram shows a framework consisting of four light rods, which are freely jointed at B, C and D. The framework is freely hinged to a vertical wall at A and C and carries a load of $1000\sqrt{3}$ N at D. BD = BC = CD = 2 m and both AB and CD are horizontal.

i) Find the reactions of the wall on the framework at both A and C, giving your answers both in components form, and in magnitude and direction form.

ii) Find the internal forces in each of the rods, stating whether they are in tension or compression.

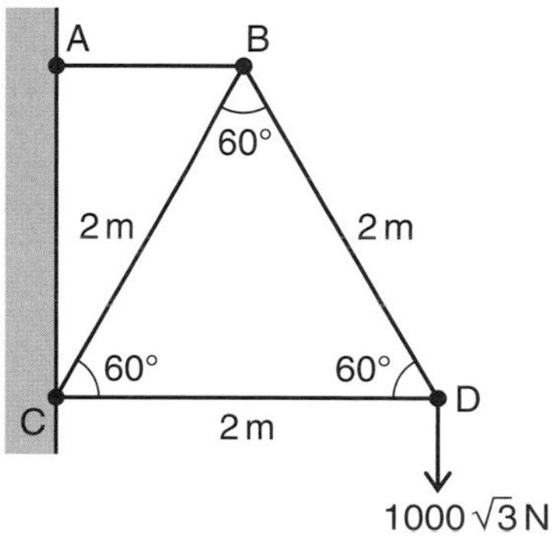

SOLUTION

i) The first stage is to draw a diagram that includes all the external and internal forces.

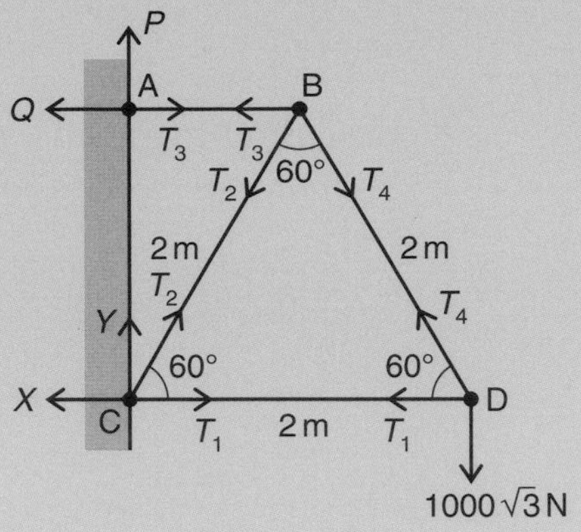

External forces

There are five external forces acting on the framework, P N, Y N and $1000\sqrt{3}$ N in the vertical direction and Q N and X N in the horizontal direction.

For vertical equilibrium (↑): $P + Y - 1000\sqrt{3} = 0$ ①

For horizontal equilibrium (→): $-X - Q = 0$ ②

Taking moments about C (↺): $-2 \times 1000\sqrt{3} + \text{CA} \times Q = 0$

$\Rightarrow$ $Q = 2000\,\text{N}$

From ② $X = -2000\,\text{N}$

> In triangle ABC, AC = $2\cos 30° = \sqrt{3}$.

Considering the vertical equilibrium at A gives $P = 0$ N.
From ① above $Y = 1000\sqrt{3}$ N.

So the answers given in component form are:

at A:

at C:

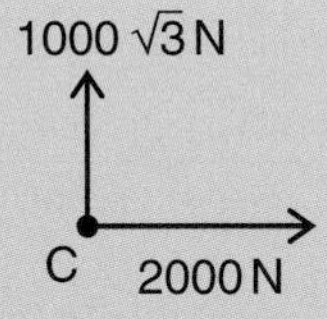

and the answers in magnitude and direction form are:

at A: magnitude = 2000 N and direction perpendicular to wall, into the wall

at C: magnitude $= \sqrt{(2000)^2 + (1000\sqrt{3})^2} = 2650$ N (to 3 s.f.)

direction $= \arctan\left(\dfrac{1000\sqrt{3}}{2000}\right) = 40.9°$ to the horizontal

ii) Internal forces

Looking at joint D

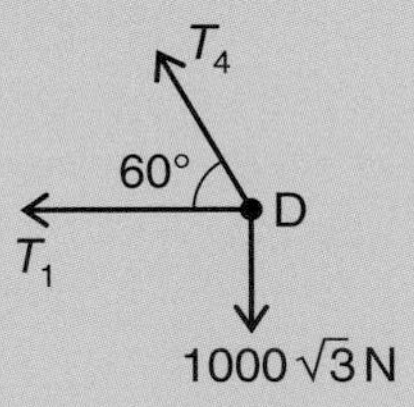

> Remember that $\sin 60° = \dfrac{\sqrt{3}}{2}$ and $\cos 60° = \frac{1}{2}$.

Vertical equilibrium: $T_4 \sin 60° = 1000\sqrt{3}$

$\Rightarrow$ $T_4 = 2000$ N (tension)

Horizontal equilibrium: $T_1 + T_4 \cos 60° = 0$

$\Rightarrow$ $T_1 = -1000$ N (compression)

Looking at joint B

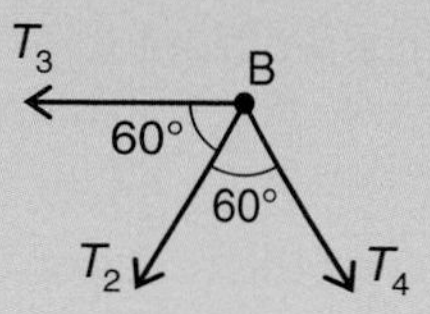

Vertical equilibrium: $T_2 \cos 30° + T_4 \cos 30° = 0$

$\Rightarrow \quad T_2 = -T_4$

$\Rightarrow \quad T_2 = -2000\,\text{N}$ (compression)

Horizontal equilibrium: $T_3 + T_2 \cos 60° - T_4 \cos 60° = 0$

$\Rightarrow \quad T_3 - 1000 - 1000 = 0$

$\Rightarrow \quad T_3 = 2000\,\text{N}$ (tension)

So the answer to part **ii)** is that rod AB has a tension of 2000 N, rod BD a tension of 2000 N, rod BC a compression of 2000 N and rod CD a compression of 1000 N.

LINKS

There are no further extensions to this topic within the A level course, but the basic concepts are developed in the study of structures in engineering courses.

Test Yourself

1 The diagram shows a framework made up of three light rods which are freely jointed at A, B and C. AB = AC = 2.5 m and BC = 3 m. The framework rests on two smooth supports at B and C and supports a load of 1200 N at A.

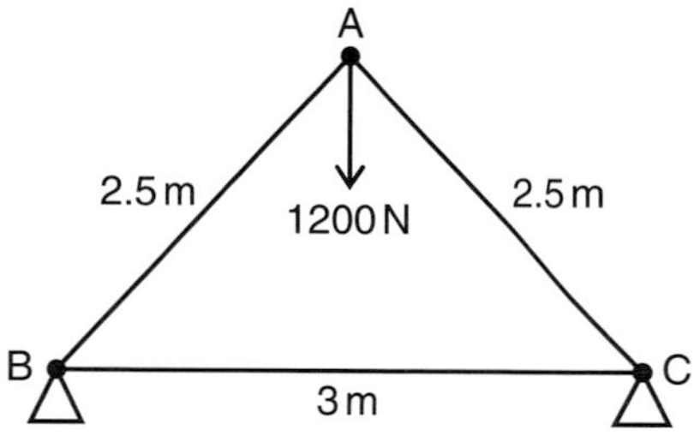

Find the internal force in the rod AB and state whether it is in tension or compression.

A 750 N, compression **B** 750 N, tension

C 1000 N, compression **D** 1000 N, tension

2 The diagram shows a framework ABC of light, freely jointed rods, each of length 80 cm, in the shape of an equilateral triangle. A 400 N weight is suspended at C. The framework is hinged at A to a smooth vertical wall and is in equilibrium with B vertically below A. Assume that the rod is in contact with the wall only at the points A and B.
Find the magnitude and direction of the reaction at A.

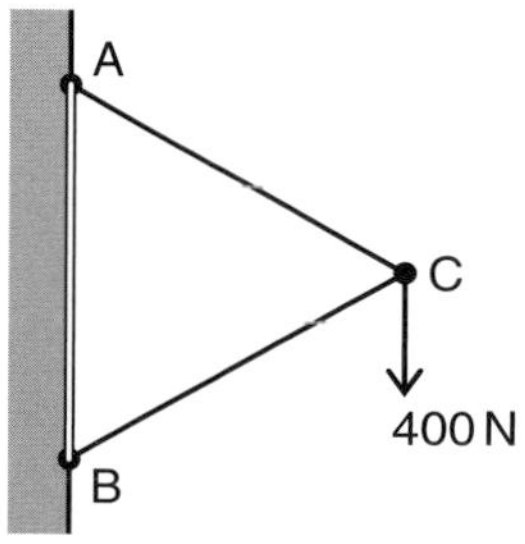

A Magnitude $200\sqrt{7}$ N at an angle of 40.9° to the horizontal.

B Magnitude $200\sqrt{7}$ N at an angle of 49.1° to the horizontal.

C Magnitude 280 000 N at an angle of 49.1° to the horizontal.

D Magnitude $200\sqrt{3}$ N at an angle of 0° to the horizontal.

3 The diagram shows the external and internal forces on a crane, which is supporting a load of 1000 N. The framework is constructed from light rods, which are freely jointed, and it is secured to supports at points A and C. AC = CB = 150 cm, angle ACB = 110° and AC is horizontal. Which one of the following statements is true?

A The reaction R at A is 342 N and the reaction S at C is 1342 N, both vertically upwards and to the nearest 1 newton.

B As ABC is an isosceles triangle the forces in the rods AC and BC will be the same.

C The rod AB is in compression.

D If the load is doubled to 2000 N all the external and internal forces will be doubled.

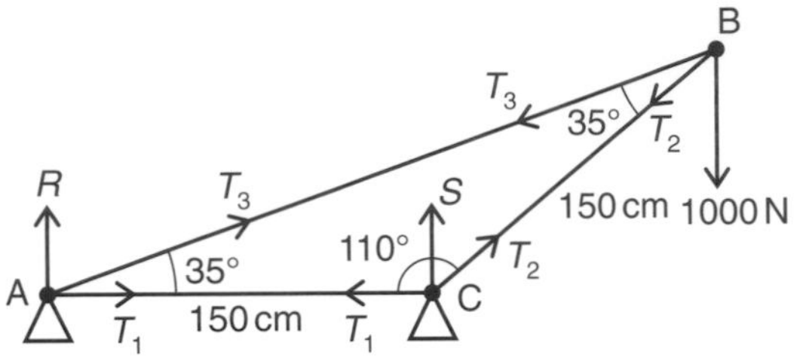

Exam-Style Question

The diagram shows a framework, which is in the shape of a rhombus ABCD and is constructed from five light rods freely jointed together. The rods AB and DC are horizontal and the angle BAD is 60°. The framework rests on two smooth supports at A and B and supports loads of 1200 N and 1800 N at the points C and D respectively.

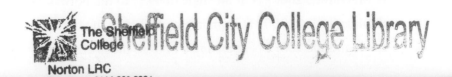

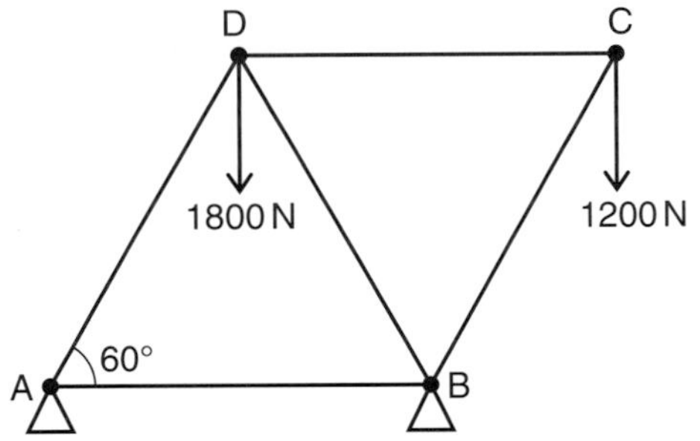

i) Draw a diagram marking in all the external forces acting on the framework.

ii) Show that the supports at A and B exert forces of 300 N and 2700 N vertically upwards on the framework.

iii) Copy your diagram from part **i)** and mark in all the forces, both external and internal, acting on the framework.

iv) Calculate the magnitude of the internal forces in the rods and state for each rod whether it is in tension or compression (you may find it helpful to leave surds in your answers).

The loads at C and D are now replaced with new loads. The reactions at A and B are now 600 N and 1800 N respectively.

v) Find the new loads at C and D.

Index

Formulae and results

Friction

Friction acts against a tendency for one surface to slide over another.

$F = \mu R$ dynamic friction when sliding takes place

$F \leq \mu R$ static friction when no sliding takes place
μ is the **coefficient of friction**.

Work, Energy and Power

The work–energy principle: The total work done by all the forces acting on a body is equal to the increase in the kinetic energy of the body.

Work done by a constant force, $W = F(s \cos \theta)$
$= (F \cos \theta)s$

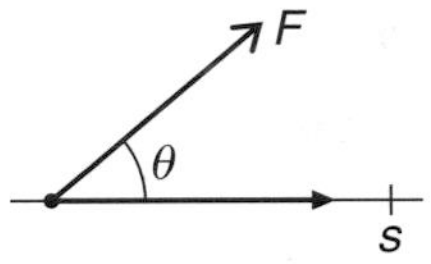

Kinetic energy $= \frac{1}{2}mv^2$

Work done against gravity $= mgh$

Power $= \frac{dW}{dt} = Fv \cos \theta$

Impulse

Impulse $= \mathbf{F}t$ for constant $\mathbf{F}$

Impulse $=$ Change in momentum $= m\mathbf{v} - m\mathbf{u}$

Impacts

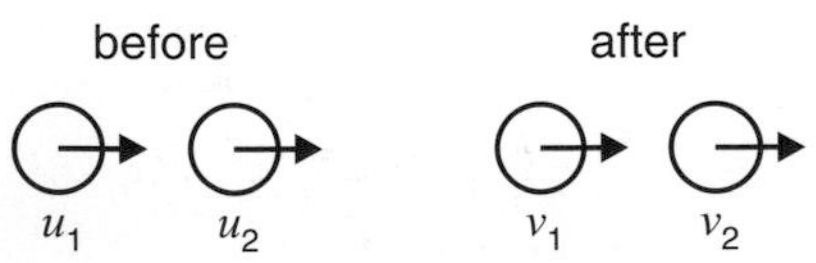

Newton's Experimental Law (sometimes called Newton's Law of Impact)

$$v_2 - v_1 = -e(u_2 - u_1)$$

where e is the coefficient of restitution.

$$e = \frac{\text{speed of separation}}{\text{speed of approach}} = \frac{v_2 - v_1}{u_1 - u_2}$$